LAST CHRISTMAS

LAST CHRISTMAS

Memories of Christmases Past and Hopes for Future Ones

Curated and introduced by
Greg Wise and
Emma Thompson

Quercus

First published in hardback in Great Britain in 2019 by
Quercus Editions Ltd

This paperback published in 2020 by

Quercus Editions Ltd
Carmelite House
50 Victoria Embankment
London EC4Y 0DZ

An Hachette UK company

Introduction © 2019 Greg Wise and Emma Thompson

Contributions © Please see p. 242

Print on p. 233 © Paloma Varga Weisz

A CIP catalogue record for this book is available
from the British Library

ISBN 978 1 52940 423 4
Ebook ISBN 978 1 52940 421 0

10 9 8 7 6 5 4 3 2 1

Designed and typeset by EM&EN
Printed and bound in Great Britain by Clays Ltd, Elcograf S.p.A.

Contents

INTRODUCTION

We started working on the story of our film *Last Christmas* about eight years before we filmed it. In a nutshell, it's the story of a messed-up girl learning how to use her heart properly. It was a long process (it always is), trying to weave a storyline and into it knit important things we felt were darkening the world. Principally, we were witnessing a growing intolerance of 'the Other' – foreigners, refugees, the homeless, vulnerable minorities, the marginalised. One of us was born to a Central European mother of Jewish extraction, who found a safe haven in England before the outbreak of the Second World War; our son is a refugee from Rwanda; and, as everyone else in our country, we cannot help but be shocked by the rise in homelessness.

We were approached by Greg's publishers, Quercus, to see if we were interested in putting together a book to tie in with the release of our film which could collate people's personal memories of past Christmases and their hopes for future ones. And as truth is, indeed, stranger than fiction, the stories that arrived mirrored what we were trying to explore in our film – our suspicion is that this collection of writings, more than simply being amusing or touching about Christmas, shows that we are all essentially the same. This is by no means a new thought, but it is worth reminding ourselves that whether we are a refugee, a homeless person, a charity worker, a vicar, comedian, doctor, beautician, actor or journalist, we share the same hopes. Hopes that we often solely hang on this particular time of the year.

Oddly, this book, based as it is on a religious festival, is more than anything a book about humanity.

It must be a rare thing to have such a wide selection of participants from such a wide array of countries addressing a single day in the year. These stories come from Iraq, South Sudan, Myanmar, Palestine, East Africa, Syria, the UK, the US. Their authors range from a reverend, 'for whom Christmas is part of the day job', to a Bible-studying child brought up to believe that Christmas 'was very wrong and something that would make God angry', to a young Muslim girl in Britain desperate for a chocolate Advent calendar and fighting her parents' view that 'Christmas was a one-way ticket to damnation'.

There are so many ways of experiencing Christmas. For some, mainly in the global South, Christmas brings with it the only new clothes or perhaps the only meat eaten that year and it is a time for genuine celebration. But many of the stories from the North are much less celebratory. They address the commercial, the cynical excess, the teaching our children of 'desire and rampant gratification'. What perhaps connects all the stories is the idea that a birth 2000 years ago brought extraordinary change. The Christ Child brought hope, as all children inspire the same hope in their parents. That, though our own Christmases as children may have been '*joy obliter-ated*', now we want our children to have '*the dancing lunacy of Christmas joy, the comfort, the giddiness*'.

But the hopes for change are far more than just a parent's wishes for a child. We see from Myanmar: '*What does Christ-mas mean when you have been living in a camp your whole life? What does hope mean for the people who are not hearing Christ-mas carols but the sounds of guns and bombs, and every day is purely about survival?*' What hope can the Christ story bring to a persecuted Christian minority?

In those writings we get a glimpse of the universal aspect of this '*story of displacement, where Mary and Joseph are forced to leave home, and give birth in a strange place in a simple manger . . . Then, on the run from authoritarian rule, they become refugees.*'

The Christ birth story is our story. The marginalised, the dis-possessed, the homeless and the refugees, are at the heart of this tale. '*Christmas challenges each of us . . . to refuse to be ruled by fear and tribalism, to reach out and connect to those who are not like us and to give up our power, privilege and position.*'

Power, privilege and position can melt away surprisingly and horrifyingly easily, and we see just how delicate is the thread knitting us into our families and society – how easy it can be to find ourselves dispossessed, even in our own country – '*I had a six-figure salary, two homes . . . I was invin-cible and never in my wildest nightmares could I have imagined that somewhere later in my life, I would be destined to become homeless.*'

There but for the grace of God go we . . .

Christmas can embody the stark reality of one's life – '*My longest, loneliest days are during the Christmas period*'. For those who have escaped persecution in another country, the pain of loss cannot be forgotten – '*thoughts of Christmas being a family day return, I drown in sorrow and tears begin to roll down my cheeks*'. For the homeless on our own streets – '*Many guests walk in hunched up, cold, hungry and frightened. The centres allow our guests to step off the treadmill, sit down and re-evaluate their lives. When they leave, they look taller, smarter and their backs are straighter. They've had a haircut and had their nails cleaned. They feel ready to take on the world again.*'

It's about the CARE – to bring someone to a place where '*it had taken almost fifty years but at last I truly understood what Christmas was all about*'.

It's about HOPE – that we can end people sleeping on the streets; to be able to spend '*quality time with my family, being clean and sober and being able to enjoy and remember it*'.

It's about LOVE – '*It's free, the more you give the more you get back . . . and I'm told it's available all year round.*'

That's the thrust of all these writings – that the care, the hope, the love alongside all the fun, the family, the connection, the giving-and-receiving don't need to be saved up for just one day of the year, but can be spread across the remaining 364 days.

The stories are arranged alphabetically by author (by first name) and we have placed a short biography of each contributor at the end of the book. Some people did not want to have their particulars included, as they are victims of abuse, or have had to flee as refugees in fear for their lives, and in those cases we have made up a brief biography to protect their true identities.

It has been an extraordinary privilege to put this book together and to reach out to people who, in the main, are not writers, and ask them for their stories. We have entered into correspondence with amazing folk, from all corners of this world, with English as their second, if not third language, and over time helped them hone their offerings. We have tried, as much as possible, to retain the 'voice' of our contributors, not to become over-exercised with grammar, idiom, syntax, but rejoicing in another's unique use of our language.

We are eternally grateful to everyone who contributed – we know almost every one of them, or they are only one-degree-of-separation from us – either via a family member, friend or someone we have worked alongside. Our hope is that you will be able to see something of yourself within the covers of this book and may even be able to recognise your own story echoed in another's words. Here, we are all the same.

All the money earned from this book goes straight to charities helping refugees and the homeless, so an enormous thank you for your purchase.

Greg Wise & Emma Thompson
June 2019

ADEL BOTTERILL

Before I came to Crisis, I was so intoxicated every Christmas season that I was oblivious to what was happening in the world. I just switched off from everyone and everything. I lost myself in television soaps. The ad breaks in between – showing families celebrating together and all the presents you could buy – were torture. I hated everything about it. It got worse in the build-up to Christmas, so I kept on drinking . . . the more the better. My family never bothered me, and I didn't hear anything from them, no contact at all. On Christmas Day itself I had no decorations up, and no Christmas lunch. It was just me, alcohol and the television.

I lost my father at three months old and was in and out of care from the age of five. Then my mother remarried, and my stepfather was forever battering me and my brother. My mother was always in the refuges, always running away. I never knew how long I would be in any home or school and as soon as I made friends I would have to leave. That's all I knew, just care, and looking after my little brother. By the age of eight, I was going on twenty-eight.

It was a horrible childhood, but somehow I managed to pull myself out of that. I grew up, got married young and had three beautiful children. After my marriage broke down, I remarried, which unfortunately didn't work out well, and I fell into a cycle of abusive relationships. It was then that my drinking started and when I lost my brother to suicide when he was twenty-four, it went out of control. I didn't care for myself and everything fell apart. I lost my family, my home, my freedom. My life was a cycle of homelessness, drinking and deteriorating health. I ended up in prison.

The only support I had from prison was through the chaplaincy, but this wasn't always available. In my last week there, I wasn't allowed to see the chaplain. It was just 'off you go', and that's how I ended up on the streets again. They used to give people leaving the men's prison a sleeping bag and a tent. I didn't even get that.

I started using Crisis services when I had just started to get sober. I had been discharged from hospital having been admitted for liver failure. The staff said they didn't know how I was still alive with the damage I had caused myself with drinking. Working with Crisis I was able to remain sober, get my own flat and rebuild relationships with one of my daughters, her wife and my grandchildren.

I began volunteering for Crisis at Christmas and it opened my eyes. What struck me was the number of homeless people left out there still without a shelter. I have been in prison at Christmas but being homeless at that time is worse. It's horrific. Crisis at Christmas keeps people safe and gives them something to look forward to. The money raised there helps more people towards their first steps in ending their home-lessness.

Christmas is a terrible time of the year for anybody who is homeless or has an addiction, and Crisis gives these people a chance to meet with those from their own and other communities. When we meet it is like our own special family. People feel included and it gives them a chance to feel like a real person who is not ignored.

This year I was asked to head up the Christmas Arts and Crafts work as the volunteer decorations co-ordinator. This gave me a sense of pride and involvement which is something I have not felt in many years. I had a purpose and for the first time I felt listened to.

I hope that the people I've met at Crisis carry on there and that they're able to get the help they need to set up a home and a solution to their addiction, to really improve their health. I hope that if I see the same faces next year, they will be telling me they've been able to put up their own Christmas trees in their own homes. That they are working on their own perfect Christmases.

Nowadays Christmas for me is all about the excitement and the preparations, which includes choosing my own decorations and putting up my own tree in my own home. But more importantly it means spending quality time with my family, being clean and sober and being able to enjoy and remember it. I love seeing the enjoyment on my grandchildren's faces. It's a very special time for me.

Last Christmas

Everybody has their own vision of what a perfect Christmas should be. For some, it's just about having a roof over one's head. Ideally, we should not need Crisis at Christmas. Everyone should have a place to call home.

AIMEE MULLINS

My childhood memories of Christmas Day itself are rife with the realities of not-uncommon family stress – parental marital tension, their financial anxieties, the hell (pun intended) of having to go to church in an outfit that required itchy stockings and patent-leather shoes. When I consider that I still get excited by the approach of each Christmas season, I realise that this flame I carry for a certain holiday spirit is rooted in memories of Christmas Eves spent at my Grammy's house.

My mother is one of eleven children. Thanks to the rhythm method, the only Catholic church-approved mode of contraception, my grandmother was consistently pregnant for two decades. She had her last child the same month as her first child was having *her* first child. As a result, we took hand-me-downs to new heights!

My personal rejection of Catholicism notwithstanding, the failure of the rhythm method as effective birth control resulted in the overwhelmingly positive experience of growing up as part of a loving extended family. And although I have eight aunts who all took the last names of their husbands, when they gather together (as they so regularly do, for anything), they aren't 'The Mullinses' or 'The Simpsons' or 'The Greenes' or

'The Doyles' or 'The Meolis' or 'The Metzes' or 'The Dussing-ers' or 'The Scannells' or 'The Fallers'. No, our family is known by the sisters' maiden name: The Anthonys. It's a clan, but we're not Scottish. It's a gang, but we're not city folk. It's just a huge family, and nearly all live within fifteen minutes of my maternal grandparents' house in Coplay, Pennsylvania.

As kids, we all saw each other multiple times per week. If my cousin Billy (six years my elder) had a violin recital on a Wednesday night, forty people would show up from our family alone. If my cousin Jason (twelve years my junior) had a Friday night basketball game, it was the same thing. When, at age eight, I played an urchin with no lines in *Oliver!* at the Civic Little Theatre, I had my own personal cheering section taking up most of the stalls. And, like many families that were cash-poor, they were sentiment-rich. The Anthonys bring it.

So on Christmas Eve every year, we would arrive at Gram-my's home, fashioned of local brick with mortar made from the cement factory where my grandfather worked for decades in the neighbouring, aptly named hamlet of Cementon. My grandfather had built the 1506-square-foot house with his own hands in the early 1950s.

The front porch proffered a straggle of freezing smokers as the first members of the family to be greeted with a hug and a kiss, as is Anthony family tradition. Stalwarts included my Uncle Jimmy who always seemed to be having the best time, both Uncle Bills, my Uncle Jack and the eldest of the sisters, Aunt Tina, widowed at twenty-six when she was a young mother of two. At some point during the evening, my mom would sneak out there for a half hour and maintain that she was 'only talking!' even though my brothers and I knew better, thanks to our allergies.

The kitchen was Command Centre for all the women, where Grammy Anthony held court. I now understand how tiny that kitchen actually was, but it always seemed to expand to hold whoever wanted to join the table, especially if you didn't mind perching on someone's knee or perching on the percher's knee (nobody minded). This is the oval table upon which my grandmother, born in the US to Austrian immigrants, would stretch homemade phyllo dough to cover the entire table for her homemade apfelstrudel. This was the table around which, a week before, my grandmother and all the sisters and the two sisters-in-law and whichever cousins would join, gathered to make Christmas cookies en masse while listening to waltzes and polkas playing on the local radio station, interspersed with Nat King Cole and Eartha Kitt. In addition to the usual kinds of American cookies (chocolate chip, sugar), there were the nods to the old country: the 'Nut Tassies', and – my favourite – 'Kipfels', small rolled cookies combining a shortbread dough with a filling of either apricot or 'lekvar', a purée of prunes. (I pretended not to know about that prune fact when delighting in their deliciousness.) It was a kitchen where I watched my father, himself an immigrant from Ireland, stave off his own holiday hauntedness and homesickness by accepting a multitude of sisterly fingers pushing the latest round of baked hors d'oeuvres straight from the oven into his mouth. He would burn his tongue every time and go back for more, like all of us.

Thanks to Aunts Rosemary and Monica, there was always a daintily decorated tree in the living room next to the kitchen. The house had three small bedrooms: one used to pile winter coats on the bed, one for the flux of various cousins watching/walking out on *It's A Wonderful Life*, and another for urgent, clandestine conversations plotting resolutions to teenage dramas.

And down some steep and narrow steps was what seemed to us kids a humungous basement echoing the footprint of the ground floor. It's where we would head first, to drop off our myriad gifts for the family. There would be a wood fire blazing in the hearth, even though the collective body temperature already made it sweltering down there. There was a second, more pedestrian tree – the 'kids' tree' – in this basement, around which all the best things happened on this night. It was a distant corner island buffeted by probably one hundred ribboned boxes and the like. 'A hundred?!' you say? Indeed. Usually the Anthony family were pros at making a little go a long way. A typical birthday celebration saw one homemade layer cake servicing the multitude of people who had birthdays that month, as we lit and relit the candles for each person's 'Happy Birthday' serenade. But the necessary frugalities of the rest of the year were shelved at Christmas time, and the Anthonys pulled out all the stops.

Our family had a dizzying Christmas gift-giving structure: each family brought a present (usually food-based) for the other ten families. We went in with The Dussingers and gave every other family a cheesecake. The Metzes gifted German wine. The Simpsons handed out hampers teeming with breakfast croissants, bagels and homemade jams. Basically you were set for weeks of holiday eating and drinking, no matter what time of day or how many guests dropped in.

Each godchild brought presents for each of their godparents (an aunt and uncle in the family) and the godparents brought a present for their godchildren (my mom had three godchildren, so start counting the hours spent wrapping . . .). Each cousin had drawn a name from a hat at the previous Thanksgiving, which would be your 'Pollyanna', basically the recipient to your Secret Santa. Pollyanna gifts had to cost less than $20 and you, ahem, weren't supposed to know whose you were. (Trades were inevitably made among the cousins to avoid the few lame-o bummers who gave thoughtless gifts.)

The adult couples also had Pollyannas (are you picturing just how many gifts we had to shop/wrap/haul from the car and nestle into this packed basement?). Lastly, each family brought something for my grandparents, and my grandparents had a Christmas envelope for each adult child and their spouse, and an envelope with a crisp new $10 bill in it for each grandchild, announced in descending order of age. This, from the pensions of a seamstress and a retired cement worker with nearly a dozen children, dozens of grandchildren and eventually dozens of great-grandchildren, not that there was any discerning between the latter two. I remember the anticipation of being called up in front of everybody for that envelope with my name on it carefully written in cursive, kissing both my grandparents, then tucking my loot into my father's jacket breast pocket for safekeeping until later.

For dinner, you could help yourself to the pot-luck smorgasbord consisting of Uncle Terry's roast beef, garlicky smoked ham with strong mustard, Aunt Lisa's baked beans, krautknockerl (I just discovered in looking up the spelling of this Austrian caramelised-cabbage-and-pasta dish that it is in fact called 'krautfleckerl'. We've apparently been using the wrong word for generations!), my mom's scalloped potatoes, Aunt Geri's barbecue chicken, Aunt Niecey's pasta salad and, of course, those aforementioned cookies. Good luck trying to find a seat.

After most people had finished eating, sheet music was passed around, although we all knew the carols by heart. A new boyfriend or girlfriend 'brought home' that year – obviously no small milestone – was teased with an expectation of an *a cappella* carol performance. Uncle Greg donned a Santa hat and employed the younger kids to be his elves to hand out the presents, because the pile was too deep and the pandemonium too great to go unconducted.

Everyone claimed a small patch of carpet, or a knee, and stayed put as their presents came to them via a delivery toddler. When all the presents were out, Uncle Greg blew a little bugle, and the unwrapping began, feverishly for the kids, delicately for the aunts who would re-use the paper. The night would end with fathers having to find kids passed out in heaps, hoisting them over their shoulders and out into the first hours of a frosty Christmas morning to find the car.

The Anthony house was sold after the death of Grammy Anthony in 2013 (Grandpop died thirteen years earlier), and those raucous Christmas Eves don't happen anymore. The aunts are their own matriarchs now, and like myself, my cousins have moved farther afield, and we all agree we don't need any more 'stuff'.

It was never about the stuff anyway; strip away the $10 envelope, the dangly Pollyanna earrings and the reams of colourful paper and ribbons, and the memory of Christmas Eve isn't diminished in the slightest. That night was about feeling welcomed and loved, and being joyous with many people.

Last Christmas, the gifts my husband and I gave each other were without any wrapping: those of time slowed down, presence of mind . . . and a homemade fish pie that took all day to make and tasted like it too.

ASHLEY COLLISHAW

What does Christmas mean?

I grew up in a home where we didn't really do God. It was always a bit of a surprise when my parents each Christmas morning would insist on the once-a-year church attendance, 'to remind ourselves what it's all about'. The parish church was simple, the service unfussy, but there was always a sense that somehow it mattered; there was a weight to it that I couldn't explain. Perhaps that was the seed within me that grew into adult faith on the other side of teenage rebellion.

Now I find myself well into my second decade as a professional Christian, a 'reverend', for whom Christmas is part of the day job, and yet the weight of the season has never diminished. It still holds magic and meaning.

The strongest evidence points towards Jesus actually being born in the autumn. It was the early Christians who decided to locate the festival of Jesus' birth in midwinter. A midwinter celebration was a theological choice in keeping with an understanding of God rooted in a Jewish mindset.

For the Romans the day ran from midnight to midnight, but for Jews it has always begun and ended at sundown, because the journey of life, and the work of God, in us and in creation, is constantly moving from the darkest point into the light. From winter to spring and onward.

Midwinter-Christmas tells me that God is always to be found where we currently are. No matter what we struggle with, no matter how dark we feel it is, God does not stand off until we are better people, until we are somehow worthy of his attention. He gets down in the crap with us.

God in Jesus is born in a stable, surrounded by the noise, muck and shit of real life, to an unmarried couple at the bottom of the social order, in a country under foreign occupation. Jesus blows away the idea that there is somehow a bright, clean, shiny sacred space for religious things to take place in, and a dirty, grubby everyday space for secular things that God won't touch. In the darkest hour, he meets us in the midwinter, and in doing so he drives us into relationship and community.

All of us, whatever our beliefs, are capable of unimaginable acts of kindness. We are wired to have compassion, to be drawn to care for total strangers. When we are feeling secure we can extend our circle of compassion almost limitlessly. But we are also at times full of fear, and when fear takes hold we shrink back into the primitive instincts that say don't trust anyone different from you, safety is only in people who are the same. In a world where the problem is often all about fear and tribalism the Christmas story is God driving in the opposite direction.

We sense this in a small way in our own Christmas celebrations. Creating spaces where moments and memories are made with friends and family. Times when we choose to be with, and bear with, to be generous with our attention to what connects us, and blind, at least for a while, to the irritating differences between us.

God, revealed in Jesus, is the one who constantly breaks through, who travels to be with us, setting aside everything he has in the process. This is the Christian rescue plan for a broken world, it is at the heart of the incarnation, to go to, and become like. To understand and appreciate enough of another's world to bridge between them and us. God of the universe, omnipotent, omniscient, omnipresent, the ultimate 'other', choosing to connect with those who are not like him by setting aside his 'rights' as God. To become powerless, vulnerable and dependent upon those he created. To become frail flesh.

Christmas challenges each of us to do the same, to step out of our bubbles, to refuse to be ruled by fear and tribalism, to reach out and connect to those who are not like us and to give up our power, privilege and position to make it happen. And this is the final truth of Christmas, that God has chosen to partner with us to restore all things, nurturing love in us until it leaves no space for hate.

Almost all of us would agree that the world is not as it should be. There is incredible beauty and goodness, but there is also a lot that should not happen, and in our more honest moments most of us would admit we are not always all that we should be. So if there is something wrong, and there is a 'good' God what is he doing about it? Why doesn't he fix it now, why doesn't he just zap it? Why doesn't he just rip it up and start again?

For me, the image of God that Christmas speaks of is of one who is committed to work with us, not overpower us. He doesn't fix the world by zapping it, not by riding in with a conquering army to batter us into regime change. The Christmas story is of a God who is happy to start where we are, flawed and limited as we may be, a God who sees the promise we have, the potential in each of us to become what we were always meant to be, and he says, 'That's where I will start. I will commit to working with you, through you, in you.' And one life at a time, one heart at a time, heal a broken world.

The meaning of Christmas is actually that God believes in us, in you and me. That there is good enough in all of us to change the world if we let him take a hold of us and give it life.

BEN ELTON

If ever I'm asked 'When were you happiest?' (the question usually crops up in those generic interviews you find on the back page of magazines) I either put 'my wedding day' or 'childhood Christmas Eves'. Clearly my wedding day is not relevant to this book but my childhood Christmas Eves certainly are.

Christmas always meant much more to me than birthdays. I'd start obsessing about it the moment Bonfire Night was over, but of course the real build-up began on 1st December: the day I and my siblings received our Advent calendars. And yes, this was in the days when all you got when you opened the window was a little picture. And yes, incredibly, we did find this as exciting as the piece of chocolate kids get these days.

In fact, I honestly think we found it more exciting because our calendars looked *so* much better when opened. The problem with the modern chocolate-loaded Advent calendar is that once the choccy's gone you're left with an empty plastic mould and a few ragged bits of foil. Behind *every single window*. The more windows you open, the more the whole thing looks like a piece of rubbish that should go straight in the bin. The

17

1960s' picture variety got more beautiful every day. It grew into an enchanting display of colourful Christmas images glimpsed through a forest of little cardboard flaps building towards the last window of all: Christmas Eve.

I think it's fitting that the calendars stopped there, on the most exciting day of the year, the day which contained no disappointment, only glorious anticipation. Because the opening of that last window (which confusingly always featured the Nativity even though Jesus wasn't due till the following day) meant many things in our house, not least of which was the imminent arrival of all the grandparents. My mother was an only child and my father's brother had no children so both sets of grandparents came to us at Christmas. And when they appeared at the front door, laden with exciting-looking bags we weren't allowed to look into, you knew that Christmas was finally here.

What a contrast they were, those two sets of grandparents. How utterly different the backgrounds and life experiences that had led them to those shared Christmases. My father's parents, Victor and Eva, were a (secular) Jewish couple from Kassel in Germany and my mother's parents, Harold and Kitty, were a Christian couple from Northwich in Cheshire. During the First World War they had been citizens of opposing nations. Victor had served for four years in the Kaiser's army and won an Iron Cross. Harold had joined the British Royal Flying Corps in 1918 at the age of eighteen. Eva had nursed German wounded (where she and Victor fell in love). Kitty had sung at recruiting concerts for Kitchener's army. Victor was a multilingual Professor of Classical History. Harold left school at sixteen. Eva loved Goethe. Kitty was the leading light of the Northwich Gilbert and Sullivan Society.

Spending every Christmas – and many other holidays – together from the early 50s until their deaths in the 70s and 80s meant they became the very best of friends. The things that brought those two couples' lives together were horror, terror and a world in turmoil. Because Victor and Eva were refugees. My father was a refugee. They arrived in Britain via Czechoslovakia in 1939.

I am writing this during a time when the world seems to be plunged into horror, terror and turmoil again and once more great masses of terrified, distressed, stateless people are on the move. It is also therefore a time when it has again become acceptable to portray refugees and immigrants as some kind of sinister existential threat – faceless units in a vast multi-headed beast. They are portrayed as an 'alien horde' who will 'swamp' our communities, like the zombies in *The Walking Dead*, massed at our borders, waiting to consume us.

But I know from very personal experience that there is no faceless 'horde', only individual human beings, scared people with the same hopes and dreams we all share. I know this because the faces of my father and his parents eating and laughing around our Christmas dinner table were the faces of refugees, the faces of people who had escaped a brutal and tyrannical regime which was intent on dehuman-ising and ultimately murdering them. The faces of people who had sought sanctuary and shelter in an unfamiliar foreign land and who had survived solely due to the huge efforts and enormous kindness of strangers.

My father was a refugee. I am the son of a refugee. If ever I need to understand the human face of the current crisis, I need only look at a family album.

I need only to think of Christmas.

BILL BAILEY

My childhood memories of Christmas are like snapshots from an array of traditional festive cards; a robin perched on a spade leaning against a shed, or a Christmas tree festooned with lights and shiny baubles. This was due in part to our kitchen garden, well kept by my grandparents who lived with us, and to my parents, especially my mother, who embraced Christmas with such twinkly-eyed enthusiasm, you couldn't help but be carried along with it. She loved cooking and entertaining, her endless generosity was allowed free rein and her strong faith was reaffirmed. She was truly in her element at Christmas, the life and soul, presiding over a large throng of aunts, uncles, cousins, second cousins and various odd neighbours, many wearing paper hats and all a little flushed and in high spirits. Often, we could barely fit into the dining room and would be crammed in around several tables of differing heights, causing gravy boats to pitch alarmingly if they were slid across the tablecloth. My father was the GP of a rural practice, so Christmas in our house often meant gifts from patients. As a small child I would sometimes open the door to find a whiskery-faced farmer holding a brace of recently shot pheasant aloft, declaring 'For the doctor!'

One of my many aunts worked for the Forestry Commission and would provide us with a Christmas tree every year. I think she was able to get one free, or at least at a substantial discount, as these freaks were the odd, misshapen trees that presumably they couldn't sell. For years, though, I thought we had the coolest trees – enormous spindly triffids with barely any branches, or round, bushy shrubs that would barely fit into the lounge. Even now, I find the regulation, perfectly shaped Christmas tree a bit dull. Our default tree these days is an artificial one that's realistic in many ways except that it's upside down. After I've assembled it, I usually bend out a few branches at crazy angles, just for old times' sake.

Some of my fondest memories of my mother are when we used to make Christmas decorations together. One year, I unwisely went solo and the result was a disaster. With large quantities of glue and a lot of tongue-out concentration I produced a Christmas greeting banner, consisting of individual letters, each one drawn and coloured in on a piece of card, attached to string and then hung over the hallway. One side said, 'Merry Christmas', and the other was meant to say, 'And a Happy New Year', but I'd made a fundamental error. I'd glued one set of letters on the wrong way so when I hung it up it read MERRY CHRISTMAS on one side and RAEY WEN YPPAH A DNA on the other. I was heartbroken but my parents persuaded me to leave it up. Partly because I think they felt bad after I'd gone to all that effort, but mainly for their own amusement. In the end, no one seemed to notice.

Relatives came and went under the banner without comment, perhaps thinking it was an old Welsh blessing.

As I got older and into my teen years, I realised other Christmases were available and spent them with my friends and latterly, girlfriends. It meant that my own family Christmas was never quite the same. I felt that, somehow, I'd outgrown it, and those childhood days were gone and with it, that rosy, traditional version of Christmas. I thought, with that bold certainty of youth, that it was time to make my own Christmases from now on. For many years after that, through my twenties and thirties, I often found myself far from home at this homecoming time of year.

One such occasion was during a trek across Seram Island in Indonesia, in the eastern Moluccas, an area known as Maluku, the original Spice Islands. After an exhausting day's hike, we were greeted by dozens of kids who laughed and shrieked in wonder at these strange, bedraggled creatures who had emerged from the forest and were now shuffling up their main street of well-tended gardens, enclosed by wooden fences.

That evening we were invited to the headman's hut, and as there was no electricity, our way was lit by puttering oil lamps. Outside, a young boy was singing quietly and strumming on a guitar. Despite the remote and exotic location, the song seemed familiar, and we soon realised it was 'Silent Night'. Many Indonesian villages in Maluku are Christian so at that time of year, it made sense that he would be singing a traditional carol. The boy was playing beautifully, despite the fact the guitar only had two strings. I suddenly felt bad that I hadn't brought any spare guitar strings, but it hadn't been on my list of hiking essentials (I always take them now). He was singing softly in front of what looked like a huge Christmas tree festooned with twinkling lights.

The whole scene was so strange and enchanting it took us a while to figure it out. There was no electricity in this village, how could there be lights? Then we realised this 'Christmas tree' was actually illuminated by fireflies. I've seen some extraordinary things. I've dived with giant manta rays, I've swum with dolphins in the warm seas of the Indian Ocean, I've seen falafels being made by hand on the streets of Hammersmith. But it's hard to recall something as beautiful as that night in Kanikeh, as a million fireflies flickered in the blue-black tropical darkness, while the soft strains of 'Silent Night' quivered in the sultry air.

In recent times, my Christmas appears to have come full circle. My wife and I host a large throng of relatives, friends and odd neighbours. Paper hats are worn, songs are sung. Mandolins, fiddles and guitars are brought out and there is much foot stamping and some whooping. I caught my dad's eye one year, and as he laughed and sang, paper hat slightly askew, we smiled at each other as we shared a moment of Christmas long past.

We have for many years dispensed with the gift-giving. I know it sounds a bit Scrooge-like, but honestly it has been a blessed relief. I always found it a bit awkward anyway. Now to all our invited guests we say, just bring a jokey present for under the tree. I was delighted to recently discover that we are just continuing an old tradition. During the festival of Saturnalia, the ancient Romans exchanged 'gag gifts' in the form of small figurines made of wax or pottery. Ours tend to be wind-up teeth and books like *How to Keep Chinchillas* but the thought's the same. I agree with the poet Catullus, who called this time 'the best of days'.

Christmas these days is often characterised as having lost its meaning and become a gaudy, glittery snowflake-encrusted spend-a-thon, the 'primary gifting period' in marketing speak. I'm not religious or a churchgoer, but I can't deny the enduring power of the Christian celebration. I find comfort in the traditions and rituals, and the way it gently leads us to consider Christmas as a time to pause and reflect.

In the future, of course, all this will be different. The primary gifting period will be turbocharged by smart tech. Our OLED glass programmable decorations will be oscillated remotely by our phones. Children wearing VR headsets will drive reindeer on a sleigh ride under the Northern Lights while drones buzz overhead dispensing gifts down our Christmas chutes. Holograms of relatives will appear in faraway living rooms to dance and join in the family revels . . . Lord preserve us.

Who knows though, there may even be a turning away from such tech and rampant consumerism. I detect already a fatigue with all that, a yearning for a simpler way of being, a longing for old stories that have simple, timeless messages.

Increasingly, life gallops along and to make sense of it, you need to hold on to a few moments, and whatever you think about Christmas, it often gives us these very things aplenty. The undiluted thrill of getting my first bike. Seeing the glorious wonderment on our son's face at his first Christmas. Watching the whole family, young and old, eyes closed, in full voice, singing together on Christmas day.

A million fireflies dancing in the dark.

BILL SCANLON

I've had a difficult relationship with Christmas ever since my childhood. I don't remember my father because he died when I was two years old. He was an immigrant from Burma and I only have two photographs of him; one of them is of the two of us beside a Christmas tree. When I was twelve my mother also died, and afterwards I went to live with my aunt who had schizophrenia, and effectively became a child-carer for her until I was eighteen. It was an unstable, difficult time. I think that my memories of most of my childhood have been somewhat suppressed.

Somehow, despite my unusual upbringing, I did manage to struggle through to gain an MSc in computing sciences and my work then shot me on to the world stage. It was the early days of CGI and I'd created a new technique that was to set the course of my career. The project quickly gained international media attention in the world of design, film and fashion.

Working in film in my twenties, I became a director of one of the four big London post-production companies. I had a six-figure salary, two homes and got married soon after. It was an amazing time and our first Christmas at work was fantastic. I was invincible and never in my wildest nightmares could

I have imagined that somewhere later in my life, I would be destined to become homeless.

With hindsight, maybe there were signs. Christmas was always secretly a time of some confusion for me. Others had long-standing family memories that I just couldn't relate to and so I always tried my best to act the part while feeling uncomfortable about the whole season, until the final relief when it was all over and I was back to work again. Phew!

Fast-forward fifteen years and things had changed dramatically. A divorce and a lack of emotional ability to cope led to a long mental slide downhill, worsened by an increasing reliance on alcohol. I became suicidal and tried to get myself sectioned several times, but they'd put me in the overnight unit and kick me out the next day. I'd turn up at A&E, and they'd do blood tests with frightening results, but they'd kick me out too. I was completely cognitively impaired by the stress, and the booze, and used to joke with the doctors that I couldn't get locked up to save my life. I was in desperate need of help, but it seemed I was never dying enough, or mentally ill enough to get any.

I finally reached my breaking point in November 2014. I was living in a hostel in leafy west London, the same borough that I was born in, with thirty or so similarly troubled souls. I had made a few new friends there. We played pool and drank our way through Christmas, all the way to New Year's Day. My plan was to get through the festive season as best as possible and start to build my new life in the new year. But it didn't quite work out that way. The drinking continued and I ended up dangerously ill in hospital just a few months later.

April 2015 marked my turning point. Finally, I had reached the most important decision of my life. It was life or death and I chose life. It took some lonely nights and deep soul-searching to finally make peace with my past and fire forward into the future. I stopped drinking, and I faced my problems head on. For some eighteen months after leaving hospital, I concentrated on exercise, nutrition and lots of work on my mental health.

I managed to find a place in a smaller hostel run by a lovely chap called Colin. It was a 'dry house' with total abstinence from drugs and alcohol and much more conducive to recovery. Things started getting better and my health improved dramatically. Then finally in late September 2016 I was offered an opportunity to move into a new housing-association flat. Even though I'd owned my own properties in my younger days, nothing could compare to the sense of excitement that I felt when I first walked through that door. The hard work had paid off and I had another chance.

As I entered my fiftieth year, something really strange started to creep into my consciousness. For the first time that I could remember, I was actually looking forward to Christmas in my new home. I was strangely excited and the whole festive season was a delight. I spent it together with my dearest friend, Eva, who'd been the most tremendous support during my recovery. It felt so naturally warm and there was no need to 'act' anymore. Wonderful. It had taken almost fifty years but at last I truly understood what Christmas was all about.

The time since has been spent regenerating my life. My little mantra is 'I simply cannot have lived this experience and not do something useful with it'. It was time to start giving something back and trying to use my experience to help improve the situation of others. I attended an event held by Crisis and quickly found a natural sense of companionship with them regarding our mutually shared ethos and approach to tackling the challenges of homelessness. I made my first steps towards volunteering for Crisis at Christmas in 2018. It was humbling to feel the buzz in the atmosphere and the amazing scale of the volunteering.

Homelessness is a deeply complex and highly personal journey. My story has a happy ending. The future that I thought, just a few years ago, couldn't exist is looking pretty damned good now. Not everybody is so lucky. My friend Andy still lives in a hostel and his health is in serious danger. Another friend died suddenly in a hostel just last year. Many of us celebrated her fortieth birthday back in early 2015. She was a mother of two.

There is a need for intelligent and informed compassion from society towards those less fortunate. Look at me: I had six years of mental-health records, so why wasn't I picked up? Why wasn't I helped? It was only when I got into the dry hostel that I even started therapy. When I really needed help, they wouldn't give me any support at all, because I was drinking. It was so frustrating that when I most needed care, it wasn't there. Prevention is a very important thing for me.

The team at Crisis work tirelessly for this year-round and I hope to be involved with them throughout the year and of course, this coming Christmas. And every Christmas after that.

CAITLIN MORAN

Christmas 1994. London.

Oh, he is a terrible boyfriend. The worst. Everyone hates him.

'He's a short man with a girl's name – and they're always trouble,' my sister, Caz, says, after she met him for the first time.

He's Courtney, and he's in a band, and I guess I'm going out with him because I think he's a genius guitar-player. That's a good reason to go out with someone, right?

'You can't go out with someone's music,' Caz counsels. We're watching him looking at himself in a mirror and pouting. 'You can't have sex with his talent. It's not in his nob. There's no such thing as . . . penius.'

But I didn't listen. As far as I can tell – because I am only eighteen, and unversed in these things – I am in love with him. Why? Primarily because he can play 'Cinnamon Girl' on his guitar, and also because he gives me a lot of challenging eye-contact. When you're eighteen, you think a man who does that is exciting – that he sees you for who you are, while keeping you on your toes.

When you're older, of course, you know what, in nature,

gives you 'challenging eye-contact' – a predator. And that being 'on your toes' is super-uncomfortable, and makes what must be your 'emotional calves' ache.

We started seeing each other in April. By June he'd moved into my flat, 'Just for a month, while I work on my music.' He immediately gets writer's block. 'You're too . . . loud. You're distracting me. Sshhhhh!' And by July he'd suggested the solution to his writer's block, one night, as we lay in bed: 'How about a threesome with your sister?'

My sister was, at the time, sleeping on my sofa while recovering from a broken ankle, and also fourteen. And, also, my sister. It was a hat-trick of 'No'.

So that was the first time I asked him to move out of my flat.

However, he had an absolutely solid reason to refuse my request: 'I can't afford to live anywhere as nice as this,' he said, looking shocked. 'I'm not going to go from here and live in . . . Cricklewood.'

The idea of Cricklewood horrified him so much he started crying – mouth open, with strings of spit stretching across his open mouth. He cried so long that, in the end, not knowing what to do, I hugged him. You hug people who are crying and sad, right?

And so, he stayed. In my flat.

By the autumn, he'd wait until I was angrily hoovering around him to make booty-calls to other women – 'Shhhhh!' – and November saw the first time the neighbours complained, after he threw a chair at me. He missed, because he had no upper-body strength. It seems being able to play 'Cinnamon Girl' does not include an effective lateral workout.

But he would not leave. And how could I make him? How can you make a man move out of your flat when you're eighteen? I used to dream of being a giant, picking him up and throwing him out of the window, shouting, 'I hope you land in Cricklewood!' If I'd been six inches taller, maybe I could have. He really was very short.

Two weeks before Christmas, my friend Pete took me to buy a Christmas tree for my once-lovely flat, which was now overrun with the parasite Boyfriendii Horribilis.

Pete is not in a band. He cannot play 'Cinnamon Girl'. He wears cardigans, and owns two teapots, and his eye-contact is not of a predator, but that of a gentle herbivore instead. He also owns a car, which is why he's given me a lift to buy a Christmas tree.

It's frosty, and I'm in a bobble-hat, and we haul the Nordmann fir up the steps to my flat. I'm still pretending that my relationship with Courtney is amazing. I'm too ashamed to tell the truth: that he lives in my flat while fucking other women.

'I can't work out what Christmas present to buy London's Hottest Young Couple!' Pete says, cheerfully, as we get to my front door. 'You probably just want "His'n'Hers" matching towels, right? Or *Four Weddings and A Funeral* – for a romantic night in? You guys!'

I open the front door.

'I've been waiting hours, you fat bitch!' Courtney screams. 'Where are my fucking cigarettes?'

Then he sees Pete.

'Oh, hello,' he says, composing himself. 'Sorry. Just . . . in the middle of a tricky guitar solo.'

'The towels sound smashing,' I say to Pete, throwing Courtney his cigarettes, then going into the bathroom to cry, very quietly. Pete watches me, silently, with his gentle herbivore eyes.

Two weeks later, on Christmas Eve, I am sitting in dutiful sad silence, eating a whole tin of Cadbury's Roses, and Courtney is pulling a pained face while playing his guitar-solo, when the doorbell rings.

Pete is standing on the doorstep.

'Christmas present time!' he says, cheerfully.

'Towels? How lovely,' Courtney says, insincerely.

'Not towels,' Pete says. He holds up his car-keys. 'You've got five minutes to pack your bags, Courtney. Then get in the car. You're leaving.'

Courtney laughs. 'What?'

'It's time to go,' Pete says. He's still wearing a cardigan, but doesn't have the eye-contact of a herbivore anymore. Now, his eye-contact is 'challenging'. 'I want you out of this place.'

'But – where will I go?' Courtney asks, aghast.

'Don't care. Perhaps your parents would love to see you, for Christmas,' Pete says. 'I'll drop you off at Paddington. Or, I hear Cricklewood is lovely this time of year. Off you pop. Chop chop.'

By 8pm, I am sitting in my flat, alone. Courtney gone. In the middle of the room, the Christmas tree shines, bright. The room doesn't smell of Courtney's cigarettes anymore, but of pine-sap. I light candles. I can feel a knot in my heart, that has been there since May, dissolve. I am safe, now. The quietness is my own, not his. I am . . . just me again.

Until now, I'd always thought that the big debate around Christmas was whether it is better to give, or receive. To be gifter – or giftee? That was the big question.

Today, I have learned there is a third option: you can give, take – or remove. This Christmas, someone came and took something from me – and it was wonderful. Someone has, lovingly, burgled me of an arsehole. And now, in my empty flat, I can finally lie back on the sofa, turn up the TV, and be me. This Christmas, I have been given the wonderful gift of being alone again.

I'm sure it's just a coincidence that, four years later, Pete and I got married on Christmas Eve.

Deborah Frances-White

My fifteenth Christmas on earth was officially my last.

Like a premature Messiah I was born on 10th December but found no room at an inn until the 20th. My birth mother, like the Virgin Mother herself, was young, unmarried, surprised to find herself pregnant and had much explaining to do. She was in labour for three days behind a sheet because she wasn't allowed to see who she was giving birth to in case a glimpse of my face changed her mind about leaving the hospital without me; in case my tiny fingers clutched on to hers and wouldn't let go. She was shown the door and I lay in my manger for ten days and nights alone without so much as a few lowing cattle for company, while it was decided by the wise men of the Queensland State adoption services what would be done with me.

The story of my homecoming was a tale I knew as well as the Nativity story itself. The phone rang. My mother answered and heard: 'We have a baby for you, but if you want her you have to come and collect her right now!' My mother phoned my father at work, but his line was down due to a ferocious storm, so she had to send him – (dramatic pause) – a telegram. 'Christmas has come early. Baby arrived. Come now!' My father's colleagues asked, 'What's happened? Have you won the lottery?' 'No!' he replied. 'It's better than that!'

He rushed home and collected my mother and sister and they had to stop at the chemist for formula and nappies because they had nothing ready. When they got to the hospital, it was beautifully decorated for Christmas. However, I was in a terrible old hospital gown and I was – (another dramatic pause) – blue with the cold, and so thin. They swaddled me in something warm and lovely and took me outside into the world for the first time.

By sheer coincidence their neighbours happened to be driving by at that exact moment and when they saw my parents with a newborn they slammed on the brakes and jumped out of the car, leaving the doors open in the middle of the road, because they wanted to find out how this miracle birth had happened. A long line of cars backed up down the road. My father would say at this point that I'd been stopping traffic ever since. My mother would say that I was the best Christmas present she ever received. I was home. I was safe. I was not in an orphanage. Christmas was mine in the nick of time.

Christmas was almost always the hottest day of the year. Despite the 40-degree temperatures that Queensland offered up in December, all the mothers in our street would roast a turkey or a chicken and boil up a Christmas pudding with lucky coins inside that you had to be careful not to swallow along with the warm, thick, yellow custard. During our Carols by Candlelight concert we sweltered through five choruses of 'In the Bleak Midwinter'. We left cold beer out for Santa and a bucket of water for the reindeer, because we felt for them in the humidity and imagined they had no time to plunge into the cold surf the way we did, after all the presents were unwrapped and all the crackers pulled.

I had had fourteen Christmases on earth when I learned that it was very wrong and something that would make God angry. The Jehovah's Witnesses who came to study the Bible with our family every week explained that all the Christmas customs were of pagan origin. Saturnalia was a lawless, Bacchanalian festival: a 'purge' where laws were suspended and 'anything' went. 'Anything' was not to be delved into too deeply for fear of corrupting our innocent imaginations, but it carried the sweat of sex beyond the missionary position in the marital bed – and the whiff of goats, vomit and narcotics. The 'Birthday of the Unconquerable Sun' was held on 25th December and it had morphed into the 'Birthday of the Son of God'. How could God approve of this merging of pleasure and piety? Christmas, like birthdays of all kinds, they explained, needed to be cancelled.

We had started attending meetings at the Kingdom Hall regularly and we took a family referendum on whether we should have one last Christmas before our baptisms into our new lives of dowdy devotion. The vote was unanimous. Five for five. One last Christmas, for Auld Lang Syne. We had to hide the Christmas tree in my brother's bedroom because otherwise the officious elders who came to our home to educate us would see. 'Jehovah can see, though,' I thought.

On our last Christmas morning we huddled inside this

assigned pagan zone of our home and exchanged our gifts.
I gave my mother a large-print Bible I had bought from
the Kingdom Hall – the New World 'approved translation'
wrapped in paper covered in holly and cognitive dissonance.
We sat down solemnly for one last turkey, one last roast
potato, one last cracker, one last lucky coin in one last figgy
pudding. That night we said one final 'Merry Christmas' and
went to bed knowing that never again would those words
cross our lips, by family pact.

I hated Christmas after that. Dreaded it. The regular form
was to go to a caravan park where families were holidaying
in our beach town and attempt to give away old copies of
the *Watchtower* magazine to irritated, merry-making tourists.
Then we'd go to the only place that was open – the health-
food café run by a local Jehovah's Witness family – for a veggie
burger and a banana smoothie. I wished I'd converted to a religion with a Chanukah or an Eid or a Divali so I had something
to look forward to – something with mysterious procedures
and amusing, arbitrary rituals. But I'd joined a movement so
singularly devoid of culture they changed their hymns every
five years in case anyone caught anything as ungodly as sentiment. I craved tradition, to be part of something bigger than
myself and hold hands with historical figures. I wanted to go
to a church with high ceilings and unknowable saints hidden
in stained-glass windows, but the Kingdom Halls were built
like Shoe Barns – ugly, windowless boxes that neither evoked
nor distracted from our unimaginative god's majesty.

I was in my twenties when I had my next first brush with

Christmas. I was nannying for a British family in America, on a trip that my Jehovah's Witness elders feared. Surely seeing the world was in danger of making a young girl worldly. Their trepidations were well founded. The less I visited the Kingdom Hall and the more I visited art galleries, theatres and cathedrals (the first two danger zones, the last entirely banned) the more I began to stir from my high-control-group coma. The elders' grip was starting to slip.

I knew that, of course, I couldn't celebrate Christmas but I was returning to Lancashire with the family and helping to look after the children so I couldn't entirely avoid it either. The family knew my beliefs and made it clear they'd respect them. They couldn't know how much I missed Christmas because it was dangerous to admit that even to myself. I knew it would be a test of my wavering faith, but one I told myself I'd pass.

The stakes could not have been higher. A Queenslander in the English countryside finds herself in a living Christmas card: a big, old house called The Snug. Real snow. Chirping robins. Touchable holly. Pink-cheeked children jumping up and down in actual mittens. Active chimneys. If Santa had come down one in front of my eyes, I wouldn't have been surprised. Everything else was real, after all.

Christmas Eve. The children were decorating the tree. I was watching, near by. The three-year-old picked up a decoration in the shape of a golden angel and gave it to me with his big, wide, excited eyes. I took it from him and my hand hovered over a low branch of the evergreen.

'You don't have to do that,' the child's father said, fearing that my employment would compromise my integrity. There was a long moment between us. And I made my choice and hung it on the tree. Christmas was mine again.

I have had every Christmas since with that same family, because if you've been adopted once, you know how to swing it again. As the children have grown up, The Snug has become something of a Yuletide oasis for other waifs and gays in the spirit of both the baby Jesus' and my first Christmas.

I expect I shall have my last Christmas on earth there. I always go and visit my mother in Queensland afterwards. I arrive late like I did the first time I came home, not quite a newborn but grateful to be in her warm, imperfect, loving nest. And then I go to see my birth mother too, who is glad I found my way back to her five Christmases ago. Because, after all, Christmas is the story of a weird, supernatural, blended family on an unnecessary journey with no firm plans but who pulled together to make it work, mixed with a heavy helping of Saturnalian chaos. In the end, the Bacchanalians had got it right.

DEREK JACOBI

Christmas cheer was rather meagre for me until 1945. I was a war baby, an evacuee, with one parent fighting a war, the other a working mum. Our Yuletide festivities were very simple and resolutely homemade, lacking any religious dimension (apart from the carols). In my mind it was a time of gentle entertainment and mild indulgence.

I remember waking up with a pillowcase full of presents by my bed, placed there, I knew full well, by my dad. The smell of *actual* and once-a-year-only roast chicken wafted around the house. Later, all our small family – my parents, the grandparents, uncle, aunt and cousin – would gather beneath the proudly and inexpertly made paperchains to play games and exchange gifts. It was a wonderfully warm, loving oasis. No television, only the King's Christmas Message on the radio.

I recall, perhaps wrongly, that snow was almost guaranteed in those distant days. And trips to the pantomime an essential. Being a London child, I was taken to the great Palladium shows where on one occasion I was taken up on to the stage by Prince Charming, played by the beautiful Evelyn Laye, to be rewarded with sweets and a balloon. (Many years later, in Westminster Abbey, I was reading from Noël Coward's *War*

Diaries at a ceremony to lay a plaque to the great man, and in the front row was an eighty-six-year-old Miss Laye. I couldn't resist accosting her, introducing myself by saying that we had once worked together. Her uncomprehending response was the epitome of graciousness.)

I've never done a Christmas pantomime myself, although the offer of Ugly Sister or Dame has been made many a time, and promptly turned down, not out of fright but out of the exhausting thought of having to perform in *three shows a day*. The urge to don the big frock, however, has never quite gone away.

The childhood wonder of Christmas stayed with me throughout the difficult teenage years and traces linger still, despite the pleasures on offer now appearing rather more garish and overblown by comparison. Too many choices, too many distractions, too many alternatives. Nevertheless, Christmas is still a magical event. Time seems peacefully frozen for a brief while and although my thoughts are not concentrated on cribs and Magi and wandering stars, my annual participation in carol services is a welcome and calming experience.

I have worked on Christmas Day in New York. Christmas in the theatre is an important time in the Big Apple, and it is great fun, but it's always an odd feeling to be having a lightish lunch and then off to a five o'clock show on Broadway where you're almost guaranteed a full house. In fact, the season in New York is quite an assault on the senses, every one of which is catered for. From the great forests of illuminations to the sumptuous shop windows, to the cacophonous clanging of the countless cash registers. Of course, we're all aware that December is a great commercial magnet (along with practically every month of the year these days), but commerce has yet to stifle the unique wonder of this particular period.

I believe that actors should always retain one foot in the cradle, be wired into their juvenile selves, able to tap into their childhoods' emotional memories and reactions. Christmas is a time when these memories are at their sharpest – trees, gifts, the white bearded gentleman, the tangerine at the bottom of the stocking, seasonal foods, chestnuts, crackers, wishbones and endless tinsel. The urge to burst into popular song remains almost irresistible and indeed, why resist? Christmas is a time to replay all of those games; charades, the hat game, finding the hairclip hiding in the book spine. We had a game when I was a child called 'Cod'em' which involved finding a sixpence hidden in a row of clenched fists. It sounds simple but often led to shrieks of outrage.

Of course, I'm well aware it can be a time of great stress. We often hear of familial disasters at Christmas; tensions, arguments, perhaps even the fights that close proximity and antagonism oft provoke. I can understand that the pressure and anxiety of organising, arranging, endless list-making and micro-managing are exhausting. But for me, the luck that has blessed me all my life has been with me through every Christmas I can remember – I've never had a Christmas falling out.

The aspect of the festive season that I find difficult is the frequently important choice of 'gifts'. I suppose an actor, used to delving into the psyche of others should be adept at picking out the ideal present (or in some cases make that *plural*) but I find it well-nigh impossible. To misquote Hamlet, I'm not good at 'suiting the person to the present, the present to the person'. But I am good at faking my own reaction to a received present that I find totally inappropriate and awful. My gleeful surprise, wonderment and joy when given the package and my welter of grateful *thank you*s is Oscar worthy – and at least the charity shops score heavily later on.

When I think of Christmas, the image that keeps coming back to me is 'family' – not necessarily blood relations (those in my case have all disappeared and even in my advanced age I feel well and truly orphaned) but a family of friends, close friends, with whom I can remember and recreate that sense of belonging and sharing and, above all, of having fun.

I will always look forward to 25th December, waking up that morning to the comforting prospect of a day of delights, a day of tastes and smells, of giving and receiving and hopefully of heartfelt laughter. It was always special and may it so remain.

EMILIA CLARKE

I would say, and I think anyone who knows me would agree, I'm more of a giver than a receiver. Christmas was always my time to shine. I would get giddy with the planning, mastering and presenting someone I loved with the ultimate gift. The entire process gave me unbridled joy, from lying awake at night going through every option and then scribbling notes before landing on The. Perfect. Gift. As December rolled round I would go into overdrive.

My dad, however, was one of the hardest people to buy a gift for. He had me stumped every year. I would spend an unnatural amount of time trying to work out just what to get him; the response on giving him something would always be that of sincere love and grateful noises but I was never sure I'd got him something he wanted, or as dads often say, needed. (I 'need' shoes and chocolate; he 'needed' food and shelter – you see the predicament.)

I get this gift-giving mania from my mum, whose generosity knows no bounds. Christmas always consisted of navigating a path to the kitchen from the tree that had more presents pooled underneath it than the four members of our family (five including Roxy, the dog, who obviously didn't miss out here either) could ever hope to open on one day.

Very quickly, our 24th and 25th December days turn into a massacre of ripped paper, ribbons and cards, presents once lovingly wrapped, now discarded in the name of all things CHRISTMAS. But throughout, my dad never really shared wholeheartedly in the festivities. The gifts for my brother and me were always from both parents but they had the undeniable trademark Mum stamp all over them. You could also tell from her beaming face as she tried to hide the sheer excitement of us jumping for joy. Throughout, my dad remained quiet and occasionally . . . erm . . . soporific.

As I grew up I was determined to get him involved and stuck in, with The. Perfect. Gift and firing up that spark. I kept trying for many years, and as my earnings went up my gifts got more extravagant (up until that point they had been a little more on the homemade side). Every time, he made all the right noises and wore the jumpers/jackets/cashmere socks all year round, but I could tell that something was missing.

Then in 2015, I had the idea of taking my family away for Christmas. It was going to be a surprise present. Throughout my and my brother's childhood we had all gone away on breaks many a time but they mostly consisted of walking holidays in the UK, or quick trips to neighbouring European countries. It had been a fair few years since we had all been away together. The family holiday had become a forgotten relic revisited only in our photo albums.

I kept my plan a secret from them all, and instead enjoyed keeping my mum on fretful tenterhooks as I insinuated I may not be able to stick around much after the 25th due to tight filming schedules (lies, all lies, to throw them off My. Perfect. Gift scent).

I waited until Christmas Day arrived. As we started tucking into a Dad Clarke Christmas dinner (he was honestly the best cook in the world), I presented them with a wrapped package. In it was a red robin onesie and inside the onesie I had hidden the itinerary for the trip to the North Pole I had planned for us. Safe to say they, Dad included, were speechless, mainly at my ability to keep a secret from them, but also at the fact that we were leaving the very next day.

It was on this trip that I realised what made my dad giddy with joy: it was the gift of us. The holiday could have been down the road for all it mattered, the important thing was that we had proper time together as a family, sharing the love and the laughs, and remembering how lucky it was that we all got on.

This would be my darling dad's last Christmas. I don't know if on some level I knew it might be and had spent my years waiting to give him this, his perfect gift, that of time. We knew he was sick but the cancer was lying in wait, we were told, till a time when it would make itself known, and I guess I wasn't very accepting of what that might look like. But this, his last Christmas, was simply the best family holiday – heck, the best holiday even – I'd ever had.

After that particular week away and after losing one of the most brilliant men I will ever know, the giving and receiving of presents – all that 'stuff' – just became less joyful. And in truth I'd give it all back in a heartbeat, every single chocolate orange, every single shoe, for one more moment with him.

So, Christmas. The perfect gift. What it all means to me is just an excuse to look around at the people you love (or the people you love to have fights with in December) and take time. Take time to remember, take time to laugh, to cry, to feast and feel alive. For me this is now what Christmas is: it's for holding on to who you have got.

EMILY WATSON

So, when Greg and Emma ask me to write a piece about Christmas, of course I say yes, because you've just gotta love them, haven't you? But inwardly I'm horrified – 'I'll give it a go but I kinda hate Christmas,' I email Greg hoping to be let off; he shoots back immediately 'We all do. That's the point.'

I've got a couple of months till the deadline and I put it off as long as I can, groaning every time I remember. And here I am at the eleventh hour contemplating why this is so difficult. I'm being asked to define myself. Oh shit. I'm not sure who I am. But I'll have a crack.

There are a lot of obvious reasons to loathe Christmas. It's so damn commercial, cynical. Characterised by advertising. Such a generator of plastic and waste, propelling that carbon curve ever upward, teaching our children to tread the neural pathway of desire and rampant gratification pushing us ever closer to that extinction tipping point. Not really an act of love. Not very Christian. Not that I am one.

Then there's family. Well we all know how that can go. The collective need for everything to be perfect turning people you love into passive-aggressive total control freaks, creating the family equation that true happiness can only be achieved through superhuman levels of stress. All this while your friends dazzle from their social whirl that you're never really in or up for. Which can all make you feel, well, low, yeah, just low.

Which brings us to the food. Oh god. Just so much to regret.

And then there's the Christ Child and every act of violence that has been, is and will be committed for or against his name. His church that keeps millions of women and children world-wide in poverty by the suppression of birth control.

So I guess that's it. I'm angry at Christmas. It seems like the poster child for everything that humans get wrong.

And yet . . .

I think about my blue watch and the walk home.

I'm nine? Ten? Eleven? We're at midnight mass in the tiny Norman church in my granny's Dorset village. The farmer's wife, Rachel, is squeezing every last drop of glory out of the tiny organ and as we launch into the last verse of 'Oh Come All Ye Faithful', I glance down at my watch, blue face, white hands, blue strap, to check. Yes, it's gone midnight. It's really Christmas and yes we are allowed to sing that last verse: Yea Lord We Greet Thee, Born This Happy Morning. And it is a happy morning. I am so happy. I beam up at my parents who are singing lustily away – even though I know they're not Christians so I'm not really either I suppose. But something is making my heart sing. We refuse all offers of a lift back to the cottage and walk home. The four of us. Mum, Dad, my sister and me. As we pass the farm, we listen out in the utter quiet for the bird of dawning that singeth all night long. I know of course it doesn't – but it's just a thing, our thing, a Shakespeare mum thing, and a thing that makes us all hold hands. The only sound in fact is our feet crunching in the frozen mud on the lane. We stop between the hedgerows and look up. It's a clear night with a deep frost, the sky vast and full of stars, logic of daytime wiped from the earth. As we stare up into the unknowable the glow of certainty starts to fade and I feel the fear of floating away. I am saved by a smell, wood-smoke, its burnt-earth embrace summoning us back to the hearth, where there will be hot chocolate waiting by the fire and we will light real candles on the tree. The bedrooms are cold and there will be Jack Frost on the windows in the morning. But as the bed warms, I go to sleep happy. Christmas Day is ahead of me, with rituals of presents and candlelit feasting to come. Life is perfect.

So what happened? I grew up, I guess. But if my children are going to feel that certainty – everything in its right place – change must come. Well it seems it's coming anyway. What kind of change is up to us.

Emma Thompson

If only we could spend Christmas alone – or with the friends we actually like, all would be well.

Unfortunately, we have for some reason all been forced into spending it with our parents, siblings and other associations that may well not suit us for more than ten minutes at a time. Days of enforced propinquity during which one is required to be cheerful cannot be good for us.

I propose a huge re-thinking of the event. We shall follow the example of the brave soldiers in the trenches of the First World War. On Christmas Day there shall be no fighting, no conflict and no memory of what has gone before. We shall meet in a neutral space, a no-man's land where the only gifts allowed shall be hugs and tears. Words are not to be spoken, thus avoiding unnecessary explanations, recriminations or expressions of affection we do not feel.

If the above sounds Scrooge-like, just think of the re-cycling we could avoid. No paper, no plastic and no unwanted gifts that end up in landfill. Just a moment of shared emotion, religious or otherwise, a moment of peace in our harried lives. Imagine it. It would be bliss.

In the meantime, all human partnerships are at some stage

– quite early on in all probability – forced to negotiate the thorny thickets of the festive season. A lot is to do with expectations. For instance, my husband would prefer to be placed into a medically induced coma from 15th December until early January whereas I start pushing cloves into oranges just after Guy Fawkes night.

Somehow, the two of us have made it through twenty-three Christmases thus far. Here is how, in three sentences apiece:

1996: Greg in steep depression. I try to raise his spirits by suggesting we cook the turkey in bondage gear. We try it, but get grumpy as bits of leather keep dragging through the onion sauce.

1997: Greg less depressed as we are in Scotland with my Ma and her best friend, Mildew, who used to be married to someone who was in Colditz. It is frozen and beautiful. I give Greg a posh army knife which he immediately uses to slice open his hand.

1998: A booze-free year as I prepare for IVF after an ectopic pregnancy. Greg depressed, so I leave beer and pies near the Christmas tree, hoping to lure him nearer. It's like living with a fucking hedgehog.

1999: Our baby daughter, Gaia, wrapped in a blue blanket, is three weeks old. We dress her up as Pontius Pilate and laugh immoderately. I sit inside the wreckage of my body and gloat over my tiny human, never happier.

2000: The miracle of Gaia continues as she impersonates an elf in the snow. Greg moves closer in as he doesn't want to miss a minute of her face as she looks at the tree and the lights and makes incoherent noises of interest and approval. Perhaps this signals a change in his attitude to the season?

2001: Greg's parents are divorced so they take turns to spend Christmas with us. His mother is clearly not a big fan of the thing. But she does turn out a good class of biscuit.

2002: Actually, so does his father. He is happy to help in the kitchen, but he is not relaxing. I begin to understand my husband's resistance to all the relentless cheer.

2003: A person called Tindy has joined the family. He has never experienced a Christmas like ours before. He stares at us as if we are all quite mad.

2004: The smoking ban has inspired Greg to build his own pub in one of the old barns back in Scotland. Greg injures himself with a hammer and Tindy discovers the joys and unfortunate consequences of sweet Christmas liqueurs. Greg's finger is mashed to pieces.

2005: Greg injures the same finger again while building a sauna. All the instructions were in Finnish. Now his bad finger points slightly to the left all the time.

2006: A true freeze this year means we have to break the ice on the river to get in for daily wash. Someone cycles down it.

Gaia and Tindy whoop and holler and even Greg is so consistently cheerful that I pray this happens every year.

2007: A rare Christmas in London with our gay mates whose warmth and generosity blow the last of Tindy's traditional and inherited homophobia out of the window. He eats an entire box of chocolates before dinner as we have forgotten to warn him of the addictive power of refined sugar. He and Gaia holding hands is the gift of the year.

2008: Greg's father has died. We raise many glasses. Greg injures himself making a memorial bench.

2009: Greg's mother has died. We raise many glasses. Greg injures himself making a memorial bench.

2010: No one has died. We all celebrate wildly except Greg. He has nothing to build.

2011: Returning from taking Gaia and Aunty Bobs (Greg's sister, Clare) to the Galapagos, we plant as many trees as we can to offset the carbon. I decide to cook a three-bird roast. Two of the birds arrive at the table almost perfectly raw.

2012: Frozen solid everywhere in Scotland. We struggle to stay warm and to keep the paths open and walkable so we can get to each other. Upon their return to London, our friends tell us it was like staying at a labour camp.

2013: Frozen solid again. Greg fashions a snow plough out of the quad bike and a piece of old roofing. Our friends have gone to Portofino.

2014: Clare not at all well again so we spend Christmas in London. Lots of visits to a bedecked Macmillan Centre. The best of Christmas spirit, that is to say, a generous and loving but anxious atmosphere, is very strong.

2015: Huge family affair with Clare and her best mate, our neighbours and all the family. We cook twelve feasts for twelve nights in a row. By the end, even I hate Christmas.

2016: Clare has died. Our first Christmas without her. We plant her many wonderful trees and water them with beer, wine and tears.

2017: Gaia breaks her special-I-never-miss-with-this-one pool cue. Greg, under the influence of Highlander Ale, immediately tries to mend it. It splinters and takes a massive chunk out of his nose.

2018: The entire family convenes up in the glen – our beloved nephews, my sister, mother, Tindy, his new wife, our neighbours, their new dog, a lot of new. Greg cuts himself unwrapping a gift. Now, I begin to fear for his survival.

GRAHAM NORTON

Catering killed Christmas.

It was the winter of 1984 and I had just arrived in London, fresh off the boat and bus from Ireland. Despite my greenness, I soon found my 'big smoke' feet and was working in a restaurant in the impossibly cool Covent Garden. Michael and Shakira Caine had been seen leaving Carluccio's across the road, gangs of brazen girls and sheepish boys waited further up Neal Street to catch a glimpse of Matt and Luke from Bros and there was a shop that sold nothing but tea! I might have been penniless but just to walk around Neal's Yard or Seven Dials made you feel as if you were at the centre of everything that mattered.

The restaurant was called Smith's and occupied a vast white basement space, where the walls were covered with tasteful art while the customers were served food that was often tasteless. A revolution might have been happening in cooking across the capital, but it hadn't reached the old-school Irish chef that ruled our kitchen. Even I thought that a special of the day that consisted of white fish covered in white sauce, placed on a white plate along with some rice and potatoes might have missed the mark when it came to sophisticated dining. Despite our culinary shortcomings, it seemed that businessmen with expense accounts and nearby offices didn't care. The place was busy and the young, enthusiastic gang of us that waited tables rushed around kicking our long, starched aprons in front of us.

As December began, some of the more seasoned staff started to drop hints that Christmas was coming and that was not a good thing. This made no sense to me. I loved Christmas and being a bit busier just meant that we would make more money, surely. The shop windows began to glitter and coloured lights turned every street into a festive avenue. This was the real thing! This was the winter wonderland that Bandon, County Cork, had tried and failed to emulate.

To be fair, when I had lived there just eleven months earlier, I had been entranced by the thin strands of tinsel that snaked around displays of knitted hat-and-scarf gift sets. I would squint my eyes so that the illuminated Santa suspended between the library and Galvin's pub glittered like the star of Bethlem guiding those wise men.

London was different. It wasn't just the lights and moving figures waving from shop windows. The city had an energy that bordered on frantic. My mother might have fussed over ordering the turkey but the shoppers on Long Acre seemed to be stockpiling for an unannounced apocalypse.

Down in our basement, one glance at the reservations book revealed that the dire warnings had been correct. We weren't going to be busy; we were going to be overrun. Tables of twelve, fifteen, twenty, all arriving at the same time. Lunch and dinner, it made no difference. For two solid weeks. The apocalypse was real and it was happening in our restaurant. We became an aproned army that had just been told we were about to be shipped out.

I cannot stress enough that this was a different time, but the rampant 80s' excess of office Christmas parties was intense, frightening and on occasion stomach-churning. My first clue that these groups were after more than paper hats and finding the ring in the plum pudding happened on the second day of the festive madness. Several large tables filled the basement and we were swamped. Bread to be sliced, champagne to open, orders to take. After twenty minutes, the place looked like *The Poseidon Adventure* after the giant wave. 'Don't run!' our manager barked at us as panic threatened to overtake his staff.

A round table in the middle of the restaurant was winning the hotly contested title of party most likely to finish the lunch slipping around in their own vomit like Bambi on ice. We couldn't open the wine fast enough. At one point, as I rushed back to the kitchen, I noticed a young woman had left her chair and was sitting on the lap of an older, overweight man. My innocent Irish eyes thought that was bad enough until I passed them and saw that she had unbuttoned her blouse and pulled down her bra so that her corpulent colleague could kiss her breasts. For some reason, this struck me as particu-larly objectionable because I hadn't even served them their main course yet. Presumably in my prudish world this was the sort of behaviour you saved till after dessert. In retrospect the most shocking aspect wasn't that they had done this, but that nobody seemed to care. All around them people were too busy ordering bottles of brandy or finding out who had the cocaine.

At the end of each night we sat in a circle, shell-shocked. Then the news would come that no taxis were available, or that there was an hour wait. Sometimes we opted to stay and hope one would arrive, but more often we shuffled down to Charing Cross or Trafalgar Square to wait for night buses full of yet more people wearing gravy-stained paper hats. If I had to design a scented Christmas candle, it would smell of sick.

Day and night, for two weeks it went on, and in various forms for the next eight years, I delivered unwanted turkey to people who were just hell-bent on having the most 'fun' they possibly could. Fun? As I watched them drink and eat themselves into dribbling fools, I couldn't see the joy. Like cats chasing shadows along a wall, these revellers would never catch what they were chasing. Christmas had been something I used to look forward to for months. Stockpiling gifts under my bed, carefully rewriting my lists for Santa, sitting with my family to watch the seasonal specials on television, but now I was just an unwilling witness to the fall of the Roman empire.

I still went back to Ireland for the day itself. I made the appropriate noises of appreciation when my mother presented the turkey. I was thanked for the gifts I had carefully chosen to fit in my suitcase, but it was useless. The joy was gone. Squint my eyes, as hard as I might, looking at the tree no longer transported me to a magical galaxy. Working in restaurants gave me so much over the years – employment, stories, friends for life – but it also robbed me of something very precious.

Catering, I want my Christmas back!

GREG WISE

My struggles with everything Christmas started early. Kindergarten, to be precise. I think the following incident may have been the tipping point. Newcastle upon Tyne, *circa* 1969. The Nativity play. A collection of tiny Geordies re-enacting the manger scene. Yours truly as Joseph. In a draughty old wooden hall that was the venue for both the pre-school and the Cub Scouts. The show was stumbling along, but ground to a horrified, bemused and tittering halt when Joseph picked the baby Jesus up out of the manger by his hair . . .

Shortly after I was expelled. Yup – you read correctly. I was *asked to leave*. I think my mother was summoned one day and gently told about her three-year-old son, 'There's nothing more we can teach Greg.'

That Nativity play was the start of the slide into my lifelong Yuletide neurosis.

I have a Christmas Day photo of me around ten sporting terrible mum-cut 1970s' hair under a paper crown. I am wearing a rictus grin, modelled on Oliver Cromwell's death mask. All of us in the picture are equally strained, holding up glasses in a toast. I am with my dad, sister, mum and gran – the only one who is grinning properly due to her enormous false teeth.

She was my father's mother, and her relationship with my mum was tense at the best of times.

And Christmas wasn't the best of times. Whether it was the fact that Gran was a gritty northerner and my mum from Hungarian lineage, and it was down to 'I'm not eating that foreign muck', I'm not sure. Probably not, as our Christmas fayre was quintessentially British – apart from the Heidesand biscuits (German), marrons glacés (candied sweet chestnuts, French) and perhaps a cheeky bottle of fizzy red wine (yes, the 1970s were like that – Lambrusco, Italy).

Maybe the battle lines were drawn between Mum and Gran for a different food-related reason: from being tiny, I would hang around in the kitchen – absolutely not a place for a male of her lineage, according to my gran – and my mum made it a tradition that I would make the Christmas cake. Maybe not as good a cake as she herself would have made, but *you have to score the points where you can* . . .

The soundtrack of the season was what kept me going: I *adored* the choral anthems I sung in my school church choir – Howells' 'A Spotless Rose', Praetorius' 'Lo, How a Rose E'er Blooming' and other rose-themed songs. Should have stuck to those, as one of the most shaming moments of my life occurred when I sang a non-rose tune at Christmas when I was nine. It was in the tiny church in the village of Kirk-whelpington, in Northumberland, where I was brought up. It is tradition to start the Christmas service with an unaccompanied solo of the first verse of 'Once in Royal David's City'. The chorister is given a single note from the organ and sets off.

Now, I pride myself on being able to hold a tune – I reached the heady heights of Head Chorister at my school – but as I got to the end of the verse, the organ started in a *totally different* key to mine. I wished the ground could swallow me up as I processed down the central nave of the church, everyone thinking I'd slipped a couple of tones during the verse. I'm sure the organist had done it on purpose. Maybe he didn't like 'that foreign muck' either.

Even though the day itself was often agony, I tried as much as possible to enjoy the run-up to it, making approximately 23,000 miles of crêpe-paper streamers, which I would wrap endlessly around my quite small bedroom. I decked the fake Christmas tree – a silver and white sparkly thing, put back in its box early January ready for the next year – with enthusiasm. Goodness only knows why we didn't have a real tree, as my mum was very much from the Germanic tradition of the Tannenbaum with carved hangings and actual candles. I never asked her about our ersatz tree – probably just a pragmatic thing: no needles, no having to dispose of after. No bloody fun. Probably the latter.

By the time I became a teenager, my parents' marriage was on life support of the 'staying-together-for-the-children' variety. And Christmas was the stage set for playing out their drama. For two unbelievably tense and angry Christmas lunches in a row I left my house, walked across the fields, on to a railway bridge and ran the gauntlet to the other side of the river, where I joined my chum and his family for the rest of the day (when I failed to turn up on the third year, he called and asked what had happened – I can't remember what kept me away that time, but I'm sure it wasn't the fact that I was having a good time). During another Christmas lunch, my mum left the table, left the house and returned early January. I still have no idea where she went.

As soon as I went to university, my parents divorced. Finally. But that set up its own terrible dynamic: which parent do you spend Christmas with? My sister and I went for the biennial option. Christmas was never going to be anything but guilt-laden, falsely jolly and something-just-to-be-suffered from then on.

And then I met my wife. She is to Christmas what Joe Stalin was to genocide – really committed. And I discovered what is meant by the 'Irresistible Force Paradox' – what happens when an unstoppable force meets an immovable object . . . Something like that, anyway. Or waterboarding. Maybe Chinese water torture is more apt, as it took some time to realise that resistance was futile. Something, someone was going to have to give. And it wasn't going to be her.

She 'gently' taught me that there are some things, actually, that are quite nice about Christmas. For example, that it isn't illegal not to have turkey, which was a profound relief as I find turkey really boring and a sort of 'poster boy' for the day itself – overblown, tasteless and almost impossible to enjoy. Over the years, we've had goose, three-bird roasts, five-bird roasts, *boeuf en croûte* – who knew that our lunch didn't have to be dry and dull? And we are allowed to share the day with people we actually like and find interesting. Who knew that was a possibility? In recent years we have sat down to eat with Rwandans, Chinese, Egyptians, Americans.

Also, oddly, despite my bah-humbuggery of it all, I now spend more time than anyone else in my family on presents, as everyone gets homemade gifts from me. In the early days they consisted of jam and flavoured vodka from our damson tree, Heidesand biscuits (the ones my mum used to make) and chocolates (from my great-uncle Max's recipe book). These days, since we spend our Christmases up at our Scottish cottage, I give folk stuff I've made in my barn – candlesticks, bowls, platters, lamps, carvings. I'm nearly reaching the point where they are tiring of timber-themed offerings. Luckily, I've found a guy who will teach me how to make ram's-horn shepherds' crooks, so everyone will get a stick this Christmas. Be a bugger to wrap, though.

As a foil to the ersatz tree of my childhood, in Scotland I now cut down a big real Tannenbaum from the hill behind us and stick it in our back green covered with lights and a big star on top. We've gone as high as 25 feet – not quite Trafalgar Square standards but rather wonderful. Unless it blows over. Which happens from time to time. The 23,000 miles of crêpe-paper streamers have become a million fairy lights which I staple all around the eaves of the buildings, with Bhutanese prayer flags weaving through the roof trusses and holly and greenery from the riverside.

I've even got over my Christmas music trauma. Since our daughter, Gaia, was five or so, I have recorded her singing carols. I put down one or two a year, getting more professional as both her voice and my ability to use the software on my computer grow. We now have an album's worth. The first recording was 'Once in Royal David's City' – her singing the first verse *a cappella*. I started the accompaniment to the second verse in, I'm pleased to say, the right key – bringing, perhaps, some sort of laying to rest of my ancient carol-based shame.

We all, I suppose, become parodies of ourselves within family folklore, with roles cemented over time, and often played up to. I am Scrooge, the naysayer, the swimmer-against-the-tide-of-tinsel, the Grump. And it's not just at Christmas. I am writing this while working in Los Angeles – a Shangri-La for so many people. But not for me. A mate here now addresses me as The Grumpiest Man Alive. I take that as a compliment. Maybe I am genetically predisposed to always be the *foil* – if I really hate it, it must be wonderful . . .

So here are the Grump's 'Hopes for Christmases to Come': can we please, finally, do what we have always bloody said we'd do and have a Secret Santa, so that we only buy one present for one person? If I am, once again, overruled, here are other various present suggestions:

- they should all be homemade; or

- they should cost less than £10; or

- they should be smaller than a house brick.

I suppose my main hope is that my son and daughter will not exhibit the PTSD that I bring to this time of year, and that I am in some way part of the joy they experience – the Infidel at the Christmas Day service, the grist to the family's mill.

I feel, though, that by the time I die, my defences (or aggression, depending which way you look at it) may have been worn down completely. Give Mrs Wise her chance – she's only had twenty-three Christmases to work on me thus far . . .

IAN RICHARDS

For me, Christmas is about compassion and caring for people who are a lot less fortunate than the rest of us. It's also about the fact that what we're doing at Crisis shouldn't be necessary in the twenty-first century. It's a disgrace.

Before Crisis, Christmas to me didn't seem to have a religious bone in it; it was all about who got the most presents, watching crap telly, falling asleep and having two weeks off – nothing meaningful whatsoever. It was the indulgence that got to me. My brother's kids were given so many presents he could rewrap the same ones the following year and they didn't notice.

Something hit me in the face one day when I was walking around London, seeing how many people were living on the streets. I thought, I want to help here.

When I started as a volunteer in 1992, Crisis at Christmas was organised chaos. We were sleeping 800–900 people a night in all kinds of donated buildings: disused warehouses, hangars, old offices, whatever we could get our hands on. One year, we had the Clapham Picture House, which was so derelict you might as well have been outside in a tent. At night, we'd set all these people down to sleep and then we'd have to wake them up early in the morning as we needed to use the space to feed and entertain them. As you can imagine, it didn't go down too well, but they still got three meals a day, some amusement and a lot of companionship.

My first Christmas with Crisis was exhilarating but also extremely sad. When you went home alone every day there was no one there who'd been through what you had. The last day at the centres was the worst day in the whole week. Once you'd cleared everything up you had to check to see if anyone was hiding anywhere, just so they could stay a bit longer. Nowadays the organisation relies heavily on volunteer welfare because there is a lot of stuff they see and hear which is quite shocking.

People think they know all about the homeless, but they don't see the whole picture. I've witnessed so many incredible stories over the years. One woman was abused by her father and gave birth to his child. She lived in a skip for eleven years and died of chronic drug and alcohol abuse, but there were hundreds of mourners at her funeral – so many people in her life loved her.

There are amazing stories of transformation too. One woman was a lot of trouble for us. If there was a fight in the dinner queue she would be there. She had serious family issues and relied on drink. But years after her first visit, she asked to become a volunteer. It was hard for her as her drinking mates were still at the centre but now she's a regular volunteer with us. She just wants to give back. I'm not sure I could return if I'd been through that.

Back then there were around a thousand volunteers, now we manage over 11,000. This year we had to turn down another 18,000 because the shifts had filled so quickly. It takes us the whole year to prepare for Christmas as it's such a massive operation. Volunteers, staff, transport, food supplies, venues, it must all be sorted. Nowadays we are given some swanky buildings like our Paddington centre, a multi-million-pound state-of-the-art school with all mod cons. It proves to our guests that we value them and makes the experience so much better for them.

We provide over twenty services – everything from massage to housing advice – but our surveys always come back saying that the most valuable thing for our guests is just having a chat with someone who calls them by their name and recognises them as a human being, not just a pile of cardboard and blankets in a doorway.

We're trusted a lot more than other services because these people have spent all year round being pushed from pillar to post, but they can come to us, tell us anything they like, warts and all, and we'll still try and help them. We're not going to fix anyone in a week, but we can signpost them to other services, and because they trust us they'll say ok, I'll give it a go.

Unfortunately, there are older people on the street who are entrenched and may die there. But we shouldn't have the kids out in the cold. Over the last four years, I've noticed more homeless youngsters and more women and it's scary because we know there are others who will take advantage of them if they aren't helped.

An ideal Christmas for me would be to see no one sleeping on the streets. And I don't see why that can't be achieved. It's in us all to make this happen.

JADE JACKSON

When I was young, I lived in a village with my parents, my sisters and my brother. My dad was headmaster of the local school and also a reverend. In our house, we would eat meat, fish and chicken regularly while others, who were not as fortunate, considered meat a rare treat.

In every household, people owned cows, goats, sheep and chickens but they only slaughtered them for market days and Christmas Day. They used the money they made from the sale of their animals and cotton to pay the school fees for their children. At that time, it was a must for children to get an education. If a family didn't send their children to school, they would be punished by the village chief. They would be made to build a wall for the school classroom or their animals would be sold off.

The best day of the year was Christmas Day. We children looked forward to it because there would be no school, lots of meat to eat and we could wander around and play.

Preparations would begin a month in advance. The men, as head of their family, would buy new clothes for their children, their wives and for themselves. The women chose the girls' outfits. We looked forward to getting new shirts, skirts and shorts. We never had shoes, but we didn't care. We just had to wash our bodies, scrub our feet, smear ourselves with oil and look smart for the day.

The whole village would cook and gather in the local school with food and drink for everybody to eat together. Later the grown-ups would use straw-like sticks to drink local brew from a big pot. Elders sat with their wives in one group, while middlemen and their wives sat in another group. Children would play, running here and there, enjoying the day, full after plenty of food.

There was dancing too. Some of the villagers would sing and others would play local instruments: okeme, guitars and drums. One person would start the song and everybody would join in, if they knew the words, or they would learn them quickly. Those in the younger groups, who had parents with a gramophone, would allocate a DJ. We would dance barefoot. After the dancing and eating, we would sleep wherever we fell because we had been so busy running around and eating, we were more drunk than the elders, even though we had not touched the alcohol.

When I grew up, my friends and I left home. We would still return to the village for Christmas. It was such a wonderful celebration and I loved being with my parents and the villagers. Our parents would look forward to our visit because we would bring bags of sugar, tea and bread from the city where we worked. I would also bring gifts of clothes; suits for my father and the elders, dresses for the girls, trousers and shirts for the boys. It was great to see their smiles.

Everything changed when the new government came to power. I was one of those abducted from our village. I was lucky. I had friends who brought me to the UK and I began a new life. But I had to get used to a new culture, the food and the people.

My longest, loneliest days are during the Christmas period. I am alone in my home. Freedom from Torture tries to help. When we attend Write to Life, the creative-writing project, we share food and our experiences. At Christmas, we are given beautifully wrapped gifts and I make sure to open them on 25th December, which puts a smile on my face even if I feel lonely. I think about my children, how they might have been if they had not been cruelly taken away from me during the civil war; about my parents, my twin sister and my brother who were also taken from me at that brutal time. I try to remember our village at Christmas: the cooking, the local brew, the dancing and the singing.

JO BRAND

When I was a child, over-elevated expectations always ruined everything. I think perhaps many families suffer from the same problem. The thing is, we never learn. I'm sixty-one, but I'm still twelve inside (that's why I tend to swear too much and behave like a child very often). My dad suffered from depression, which probably didn't help. Every annual festival in the calendar which required a modicum of acknowledgement lay across the year like a tiny trap waiting to do me over. New Year's Eve was torment, as were birthdays and other festivals which were meant to be fun.

The worst, of course, was Christmas. Every year, my father seemed to buckle under the strain of having to have a good time. This resulted in chessboards flying up in the air, melodramatic walkouts and quite a lot of shouting, while the rest of us did our best to pretend everything was ok.

So, when I finally left home at the impolite behest of my dad, I looked forward to relaxing as my first Christmas without my family approached. I was going to spend it with an old school friend, Andy, and his family in a picturesque village called Groombridge in deepest Kent. My boyfriend – the reason, incidentally, I had been chucked out by my father –

had to work at the last minute in a children's home where he was living in west London. I arranged to meet him there on Christmas Eve, planning to catch the last train to as close to Groombridge as possible.

After consuming a fair amount of alcohol in west London's bountiful array of pubs, we made our way by Tube to Charing Cross Station, only to see the back of my last train disappearing into the distance. The boyfriend then grudgingly agreed that I could stay in his bed in the children's home, something which was completely forbidden, warning me that if I was discovered, he would be immediately sacked. After a glorious night in his single bed, I was unceremoniously kicked out at 6am before the day staff came in, only to discover no transport was running *at all*. I stood on Fulham Broadway with my thumb stuck out and my Christmas odyssey began (let me just say if anyone thinks this will sound fun and wants to have a go, PLEASE DO NOT; it was dangerous then and it's worse now).

My first 'lift' looked so much like Quentin Crisp it probably was him and I just didn't realise it. He was driving a magnificent Bentley, because, he informed me as I got in, he was spending Christmas alone in his flat in Chelsea and he was already bored. He was dressed in a beautiful coat, a melodramatic hat and an exquisite cravat which probably cost more than my entire wardrobe put together. He invited me to spend the day with him. I wavered . . . what a tale this could turn out to be. But Andy was expecting me, so I declined and 'Quentin' very chivalrously drove me south of the river and dropped me smack bang in the middle of the Elephant and Castle.

There I stood for quite a while until a sizeable old geezer in a tiny Austin pulled up and motioned to me to get in.

My chauffeur was in fact deaf, but after some adjustments to our communication style, he set his sights on Eltham in south-east London and off we set quite happily. He talked at me the whole time. I tried taking part by shouting so he could hear me, to no avail, so I smiled and nodded while he told me how his family were driving him insane and he'd decided to stay out for an hour or so. Driving to Eltham and back would just about do it, he said. He talked at me for the rest of the journey.

He dropped me off at a crossroads in Eltham, which was still a little way off from my destination – 34 miles, to be precise.

Lift number three was the trickiest. An anonymous grey saloon pulled up containing a middle-aged woman with short grey hair and tasteful clothes. She was friendly enough, but after ten minutes of anodyne chat her hand strayed on to my leg and began to stroke it.

'I'm sorry, I don't like that,' I said.

Why did I apologise? She all but did an emergency stop, leaned across me, opened the car door and told me to get out, which I did, quickly. In a noisy vomit of exhaust fumes, she was gone. I felt a bit shaken, sat on the kerb and steeled myself for the next lift. This arrived in the form of a ruddy, scruffy, jolly farmer. (In Eltham? Yes, I know.) He explained he'd just come out to try and find a newspaper somewhere, and asked me where I was going.

'Right, let's go,' and off we went. The reassuring sheep-dog in the back of the car listened to our conversation as it ranged far and wide around the subject of farming practice, and before I knew it we were outside the village shop run by Andy's mum and dad. Where did the farmer live? Why had he driven so far? I don't know. With a wave and a bark, he and his sheepdog were gone.

It was nearly 5pm by then. My journey had taken almost twelve hours.

As I stepped into Andy's home I was enveloped in Christmas warmth and cheer. What a difference to the Christmases I was used to. I realised I was starving; Andy told me they'd saved me Christmas dinner and went to get it. He arrived back with a plate piled high with every Christmas food cliché . . . except that there were no roast potatoes. He admitted they hadn't been able to resist finishing them. And just like that, all the happiness I had been feeling disappeared. At that moment the fact that there were no roast potatoes was more tragic than anything that had ever happened in my life. I went into a massive sulk.

Petulant, childish, needy, ridiculous, selfish, entitled, ungrateful . . . add your own adjectives, folks. I was being all those things with knobs on. Still, I got over it after a while.

These days, as people I love gradually disappear off my horizon, I hope I have learned to value the right things and, in my case, do christian with a small rather than a big c.

Happy Christmas!

JOHN BIRD

Perhaps it is inevitable that you can't have good Christmases without bad ones.

My four brothers and I lived with my mum and dad in a Notting Hill slum. It was a house part-condemned, but at least it was a home. Although we were exceedingly poor, I remember Christmas 1952 as one full of joy because it was the Christmas before the family broke asunder and we boys were put into care.

I was six that Christmas. My dad was home from the building sites he worked on. We had logs for the fire. We made decorations out of old copies of the *Daily Mirror*. We had a chicken for our Christmas dinner, and as the potatoes were peeled and cooked alongside it, we listened to music on our wireless all day long.

There was a bounce in the air and everyone seemed happy with our mum and dad spoiling us within their narrow means. There seemed nothing lacking because it was truly peace on earth and goodwill between us all. My brothers and I were usually a warring tribe of boys.

Of course, we still had rats and mice and fleas to accompany us on our special day; and rattling windows and damp.

But we were as snug as bugs in a rug. And I can't think of any Christmas that was better than this one, despite the poverty and the hardship. I cannot think of a time when we were so fully a part of each other. That Christmas Day was a shining example of the endurance and obduracy of some of our poorest to make the most: something out of an apparent nothing.

To add to the joy, that night I sat out on the small door-step that led directly on to the street. I loved that it was cold, bitter and empty outside and warm within; and I was sitting in between the two.

Off towards the railway bridge I noticed a very tall and thin man coming towards me. As he walked, he seemed to roll slightly from side to side, as if his feet were sore. He was ever so slow, and I could see even at my age this was not a happy journey he was on.

As he came nearer, I could also see he was a dark-skinned man. The nearer he got the more massive and long he seemed. When he reached me he stopped and looked at me. He took a half crown from his pocket and gave it to me.

'Happy Christmas, little boy.'

I took it. My mum had alerted me very early in life to take what was given, to rely on the kindness of strangers. She was always begging cigarettes or cups of tea in the cafés near by. So I was not going to refuse the generosity of a stranger.

'Happy Christmas, mister!' I said in reply. He carried on walking, and I watched him as he ambled towards the main road, rolling on like a sailor or a pirate. Then I rushed inside and my mum took the half crown for the next essential item she had to buy.

Christmas for me is not a time for presents, but a time for a genuine desire for goodness to flood the world and wash away its pains. Having spent many Christmases after that away from my family in various homes and institutions for the morally wrong, and still others rough sleeping and one in A&E after cutting a hole in my leg, I can't say my Notting Hill slum Christmas was not the best and most echoing.

JORDAN STEPHENS

My late grandmother used to live in a house on Victoria Road in Brighton, about a third of the way up a ridiculously steep hill. She lived opposite a woman called Mrs Roberts who used to feed her dogs Smarties. I used to think she had a speech impediment too because whenever she said her name, she'd pronounce it 'Mishes Robertsh'. In fact, it wasn't a speech impediment, she just didn't have any teeth.

The house was like a giant lucky bag of mysterious things to explore and savour: a big old bath, dark red-patterned carpet, fig biscuits, nuts and raisins at 11am, rock cakes, *Homeward Bound 2* on VHS, the fact there was an attic. In this house, my cousins and I would be free to be whatever we wanted. That included pretending that we were cats. My gran once left two plates of milk out on the kitchen floor ready for me and my cousin Sita. We descended the stairs (quite dangerously) on all fours and proceeded to meow while we lapped it up.

There was one particular Christmas that I remember fondly. We all got to share a bed in my gran's room. The bed was massive, but there were so many of us it was like that nursery rhyme that goes: 'There were three in the bed and the little one said, ROLL OVER . . .' I had to deal with a couple of spreadeagled bed-hoggers while hanging on to the edge as if for dear life.

We woke up that Christmas morning to half-eaten mince pies at the foot of the bed and stockings full of presents. My mind was utterly blown. I genuinely for the life of me could not understand how flying reindeer with sleigh bells on them could land on the roof, before a rotund, bearded, Richard Attenborough lookalike would descend what I'm sure was no longer a working chimney and deliver presents. But it must have happened. How else could you explain the bulging pillowcases?

I can't remember what I was given. I can't remember what it was that I wanted. But I can remember that feeling: absolute belief in the impossible.

That feeling was all that I ever cared about. The possibility that not everything is as it seems. As I got older and taller, reality began to pull back curtains on those parts of life that were full of life. As the years went on, gods, goddesses, saints and deities would fall from their mantels in the name of science, adulthood, facts and responsibility. And in their place these new gods appeared on the television; forcing feelings of inadequacy so that you would pray to them; promising an upgrade of your existence as if you had always needed it; magnifying a sense of incompletion previously embraced by the endless spectrums of the imagination, and a deliberate acceptance of the unknown.

Last year, I woke up on the morning of 25th December with only my dog, Spike, a collie retriever rescued from the streets of Macedonia, to keep me company. I decided to take a walk down to the beach with him. It was cold-sunny, which I quite like. Bright enough to smile, but you were encouraged to hug yourself. I didn't feel lonely at all and for that I was grateful. Spike bounded towards the water like they were old friends. Paws pummelling sand, black fur surely designed for this climate. I looked out to the sea and felt calm. So calm, I felt a little sad. Not so sad that I didn't feel happy. Do you know what I mean? Connected, in a way. A place where everything feels the same.

And in the same way, this time of year twists and grows and breaks and shifts and weeps and smiles. For some the family has grown, for some the family has shrunk and for some there's no family present at all. There's magic in there somewhere. I still feel it. But now, as an adult, it's harder to find. The nearest that I've come to that absolute belief is in discovering a time before Christmas when the Romans celebrated the God of Saturn during what was then called Saturnalia, before religious constriction. Saturnalia was a time of anarchy, bedlam and overkill full of singing, dancing and eating too much. Feasts of fools and lords of misrule. To an extent, that spirit still lives on and it's always been those elements of festivity that I've enjoyed the most.

Who doesn't love a bit of anarchy?

That's why Christmas to me is about doing whatever you want. Christmas should be spent opposing the forces that have taken your freedoms. I will not let anyone or anything tell me otherwise. The end of the year marks rebellion. Even if that rebellion is against Christmas itself.

Back on the beach that day, Spike and I dodged around each other until he became momentarily distracted by an orange ball and a similarly excitable canine. As they burst into a game of kiss chase I noticed the dog's owner was a fair-skinned elderly woman with a wonderful perm and a dark blue jacket. I smiled at her and she smiled back. After redirecting her attention to her dog, she screamed out:

'Play nissshely, Bobby! Don't get too exshhhited!'

JOSH ROGERS

Growing up, Christmas was always a very happy time of year which I spent with all my immediate family and friends. The magic dissipates a bit as you get older, but you also start to realise how fortunate you are to have had that experience.

Six years ago, I was living in London and working in education technology, on a social learning platform with a really positive mission, connecting kids from different countries. I usually left London to go home at Christmas, but I had stayed that year and was looking at some different volunteering opportunities. It was something I'd been meaning to do for ages, and initially I was looking at mentoring children from disadvantaged backgrounds, but then Crisis came to my attention.

I was aware of the homelessness problem and had witnessed it getting worse in every part of London. I live on a busy high street and there's an alarming number of rough sleepers there. I'd got to know some of them in a superficial way but walking past them every day began to sit very uncomfortably with me. I'd realised there were a whole range of reasons why people hit hard times, but at the end of the day I was still going back to my comfortable flat after speaking to them. Crisis at Christmas felt like a gateway to understanding them better and helping more.

I didn't know what to expect when I first started. I volunteered in one of Crisis' day centres in west London and my first impression was what an amazing team the Crisis volunteers were. I was so impressed. I also didn't realise how many people did this and for how many years.

The services we provide for our guests depend on each individual. Some people simply want to come and catch up on sleep. You can't function properly when you're on the street, so just getting your head down for a week is invaluable. But it's important to engage with services like doctors, dentists and housing advice. Many of them really rely on that support at Christmas, because they can't access it at other times of the year. By connecting them with others who can help and breaking down those barriers, you're creating a welcoming and healthy environment where people can recalibrate, have a chat and relax.

It's my fifth year volunteering now, and last year I'd committed to do my shifts in October, but my girlfriend and I had also planned a trip to Mexico the second half of Christmas. We wanted to get married there as well but logistically it wasn't possible, so we looked at our local registry office. The only date left was the day before we were due to go on holiday, and also the last day I had an afternoon shift at Crisis at Christmas. I didn't want to let them down, so we decided to go for it. We got married in the morning, had a really nice lunch then I went to do my shift in the afternoon. We just turned our holiday to Mexico into our honeymoon. It was quite a spontaneous decision, but all the dates just seemed to align. My girlfriend has volunteered before so understood. It's not the traditional route but that's not us anyway. I've been to so many weddings that felt so formulaic. This felt more like us. It was amazing. All the volunteers and the shift leaders made a banner that said 'Just Married' and we all had a drink to celebrate after the shift.

I know it sounds obvious, but volunteering for Crisis at Christmas gives you perspective about what's important in life, and it stays with you. We're so increasingly busy the rest of the year and Christmas is the main time when families get together and reconnect again. Being at Crisis during that period definitely makes you count your blessings, but it's not all guilt and sadness. Homeless people at the centres are in a great environment, getting support. There's an atmosphere of optimism and positivity which gives you hope. It's upsetting on one level, but uplifting too.

It's also an amazing way of mixing people who wouldn't normally interact with each other. I can't think of any other place throughout the year with so much diversity. There's a huge variety of people with all different kinds of stories. You really feel part of something. You don't get that in your daily life and nothing else compares with it.

Christmas is a great opportunity to tap into feelings of goodwill towards others, and I think many of us want to hold on to those feelings all year round. In all the conversations I have at Christmas, it becomes clear that people really do want to tackle this crisis, but what we've been doing to help the homeless so far is clearly not enough. We're failing as a society. They are not getting the help they need, and the government has to take this much more seriously. Unlike other countries we have amazing charities like Crisis who actually have a plan to end homelessness. Of all society's problems this is one that, together, we can definitely solve.

Kate Parrott

Christmas is a time of year that, for a child, can be magical. But, for an adult, when its religious significance is often lost within a media circus of consumerism starting in September, it can easily become a more cynical experience altogether.

Sometimes, though, something comes along to make you re-evaluate your thoughts not only about Christmas, but about life itself.

I remember my childhood Christmases as predominantly happy family affairs. My parents, my grandmothers and I used to go to a restaurant for lunch then, on Boxing Day evening, we would all go to my cousin's for tea. There would be extra presents under the tree for us children including the seemingly mandatory chocolate orange from my aunt. It became a pleasant, amusing tradition.

Yet, even at an early age, I realised that Christmas could also be tinged with sadness as, many years before I was born, my maternal grandfather had died suddenly at home on Christmas Day itself.

For many of us, Christmas is a time of holidays and a break from work or school, but many medical professionals spend their festive season saving others. Although most operations are scheduled in advance, some can have no such preparation. This is particularly true of organ transplantation.

I was born with a complex congenital heart condition – a three-line-long diagnosis with some very complicated words. After years of expert care at London hospitals, ranging from Great Ormond Street to University College Hospital and the Heart Hospital, by February 2014, I was suffering from late-stage heart failure. There were times when I could barely walk from one room to another without becoming extremely breathless. I was often on oxygen at home and had to use a wheelchair when going out.

I was transferred to the Freeman Hospital in Newcastle upon Tyne, where there are specialists in complex congenital heart transplantation. I underwent a heart-transplant assessment. I went 'live' on the transplant list in October 2014 and was told that the average waiting time was two years. I was allowed to return home to wait for the call rather than having to stay in hospital, although there was no guarantee that a call would come in time. Indeed, there was no guarantee that I would still be alive at Christmas. I was literally living from day to day. I would wake up every morning and think to myself, 'Well, I'm still here.'

Being on the active transplant list meant a return to the family Christmases of old, now spent with my husband, parents and grandmother. Never did it feel more true that this is a special time to reflect on what is so precious in life. When you are faced with the possibility of losing life itself, it makes you re-evaluate and take stock of what is really important – like spending time with those you love. During that Christmas of 2014 I felt a sense of calmness, although we all realised that the telephone might ring at any time to tell me that a suitable donor organ had been found. Indeed, I have a friend who received his heart transplant one Christmas Eve.

For me, the call came in February 2015, just four months after I had been placed on the transplant list. I was so lucky – doubly so as my transplant went ahead on the night of that first call. So many people I know have been called into hospital only for their operation not to go ahead for a variety of reasons, some more than once. For me, it really was first time lucky. I felt like I had won the jackpot.

I was not allowed to travel abroad for a year after my operation, so my first post-transplant Christmas was again spent with the family. Of course, it was extra special – just being alive and healthier than I had ever been. I always remember when I was a schoolgirl and my class ran the 100 metres, I was the one holding the stopwatch and timing them all, as I was unable to take part myself. Now, I could walk for miles and miles without a hint of breathlessness.

Unbeknown to me at the time, that first post-transplant Christmas would take on extra significance as it was the last I would spend with my beloved grandmother. She died in early December the following year at the grand old age of 103. If I had not received the 'gift of life' the previous year, I would not have had the extra 'gift' of those precious Christmas moments with her.

It may sound clichéd but there really is not a day that goes by when I do not think about my unknown donor and their family. Certain times of the year, like my transplant anniversary and Christmas, tend to heighten those thoughts and memories. To be an organ donor or a family member who gives the required consent for the donation of their deceased loved one's organs is a truly remarkable, selfless act. They are all incredibly special individuals – particularly as one person can save a number of lives.

I have now been lucky enough to see four more Christmases since my transplant, spent in a variety of locations across the world. Each Christmas is an unexpected and precious gift for us and we hope that there will be many more to come. I have a sense now of really being able to live in the present and look to the future rather than just exist from day to day.

So, I would like to take this opportunity to wish you all happy Christmases to come and to ask you to please spare a thought for all donors, their families, surgeons and hospital staff who allow the most precious gift of all to be given not only at Christmas but all year round – the Gift of Life!

Katy Brand

I have always enjoyed what I like to call a Christmas tingle. As a child, I loved that special seasonal magic – gold and silver tinsel, baubles catching the light of a candle, a distant 'ho-ho-ho', and the feeling that normal life could be suspended for a few days. Nothing really bad could ever happen at Christmas, I thought. And even if it did, you could just grab another fistful of chocolate.

I was not one of those people who got cynical about it all once I hit twenty-one. I carried on loving and cherishing that cocooned feeling. If nothing else, the dreaded post stopped for a few days and all those bills – the bleakest signifier of adulthood – could wait. Bliss. Pour me another drink of that potent ruby-red punch, whatever it is, I'll sort it out later.

I shared this love of Christmas, and that Christmas tingle, with one of my best friends, Kate. She was always one to get the tree up early. She loved to cook, she loved to feed. We met at university and she and I, along with our little 'Urban Family' gang kept a tradition of meeting for a Christmas dinner every year, just us at first, and then expanding to include partners and children. We were a merry bunch indeed, and the tingle was always strong, as lamb shanks, or ladles of stew or even the full turkey and trimmings were shared around a groaning table.

Kate died on Christmas Day, 2014, of cancer, aged thirty-six. That was her last Christmas. And in some ways, for a while it was mine too – because as the message with the awful news arrived, my Christmas tingle left me. I knew her death was coming – we all did. She'd had a diagnosis two years earlier, and we had all lived through her treatment – the spikes of hopes, the depths of realisation as each gruelling round of chemo failed to hold back the onward march of her all too efficient tumours.

She wanted to hold on for Christmas Day, just one more, and true to form she managed it. She slipped away with Santa Claus early that morning. I laughed darkly – my cack-handed way of dealing with the shock – that this was typical of Kate, to leave on a day that would embed itself in our memories. There was no chance of us forgetting it. The anniversary of her passing could never slide by unnoticed in the years that followed. Kate had always known how to make a statement.

And for the next few years, all I could do was remember. I admit that I was largely going through the motions at Christmas after that. I did try: I bought ever fancier baubles. I mixed ever stronger punch. We continued with our Christmas dinner for friends, but there was a hole in the middle of it and we all knew it. We wept with her family. We raised toast after toast.

Kate had a talent for living. She was just so damn good at it – if there was food on your plate, she wanted to taste it; if there was a lake, she wanted to swim in it; if the sun came out, she turned her face to it. The injustice of her having to forgo the rest of her days on Earth was heavy. I assumed my tingle was gone for good. Why should I have one, when she couldn't? Where was the fairness in that?

But I know Kate wouldn't have wanted this for me, or anyone. If nothing else, I had a young family of my own, and I did not want to infect their early magical Christmas memories by being a mopey mummy. I had to pull myself together. Fake it 'til you make it. Or, given the time of year, bake it 'til you make it. And I did fake and bake my way through the following four Christmases.

And then, last Christmas, somehow, by some miracle, the tingle came back to me. Perhaps it was because I found myself in a new country, where Christmas is a serious matter, and the smell of *glühwein* and other assorted *leckerei* was too over-powering to resist. But suddenly, one night, I looked out of our window into the dark, and just at that moment, someone in the opposite house flicked on a switch and I could make out the shapes of an angel and star in a gentle yellow-white glow. The magic fired in my belly, and burst into my heart. I fizzed inside.

Only for a moment, but it was there.

I caught my breath. I smiled and closed my eyes. It's not lost forever after all. It can come back. It will be stronger next year, I'm sure of it. God rest ye, Merry Kate. We'll share a tingle again.

LAILA OMAN

At my house it was not the Grinch who stole Christmas, it was my parents.

We were Muslims and my mum and dad made it clear to my brother and sisters and me that 'Muslims don't celebrate Christmas'. It did not stop me from trying. As a child I would sneak a Christmas Advent calendar into the trolley when we did the weekly shop from the first week in December onwards. It was so pretty and colourful, I knew there was magic to discover behind each and every window. I wanted to fit in with the rest of the 'cool kids' at school, and join in their gleeful conversations about melt-in-the-mouth chocolates before breakfast. It was like my classmates belonged to a special club, and admission was through one of those Advent-calendar doors.

I would get busted at the till when, along with the tinned tomatoes, onions and other food staples, the offending item made its procession slowly down the checkout counter conveyor belt for all to see. My horrified parents always made sure it was a public parental teaching moment – you know, the kind that fills every child with dread. The reminder of our Muslim faith and of our beliefs was for my benefit but also, apparently, the benefit of everyone within earshot of the till. I felt ashamed but I was not to be defeated. The allure of that calendar was far too much for me to resist and I persisted in my Christmas dreams despite my parents' attempt to shame them away.

I imagined wearing a garish Christmas jumper with pride. I hated Brussels sprouts, but I would have eaten them anyway if that meant we were celebrating Christmas. And the presents . . . I mean, what? All I have to do is be nice and I get a ton of presents from a jolly stranger in the sky who climbs down my chimney in the middle of the night, and fulfils all my dreams and wishes? Hell, yeah, count me in! My eyes would pop out of my head as the other boys and girls would recite by heart the lists they had compiled for Santa.

I would have been happy for Father Christmas to bring me a skirt to wear to school. My sisters and I were the only girls in the school who had to wear trousers – boys' trousers, to boot! Girls' trousers were not part of the school uniform, and Muslim girls don't wear skirts. I don't think I was asking for much, in hindsight.

When I was ten years old, I was actually caught looking up the chimney in our house. With my head halfway up the flue, my bottom and my legs just about visible, I heard a laugh. I knew it was my mum, and I had never heard her laugh so hard. I froze. I almost wanted to just stay up there and not come out because I was afraid that she would scold me.

Instead, she embarrassed me. She told the whole family I had been waiting for Santa, and that I was 'silly' enough to believe he was real. Most parents break the truth about Father Christmas' non-existence gently. Not in my household. I was a laughing stock. Shamed and humiliated. Half of me had known he wasn't real. But the other half enjoyed dreaming about magical faraway places and elves stitching a pair of girls' trousers for me.

Christmas Day, you won't be surprised to hear, was just another day, like any other day in the year. It held no meaning to my parents, and they wanted it to hold no meaning for my siblings or me. See, my parents believed that celebrating Christmas meant we were being blasphemous towards their Islamic beliefs. Christmas was a one-way ticket to damnation.

It didn't stop me waking up and feeling the Christmas spirit, albeit in secret. I remember one particular Christmas Day we were so lucky, we woke up to a magical white Christmas, ankle deep in snow. It was like something out of a movie, so utterly magnificent. My siblings and I got to play in the back garden and build a snowman. It had a carrot nose that we stole from the fridge. It even had a Man United scarf. Oops, not very Muslim of us, I know.

I now think I was mis-sold Christmas by my parents, but also by my classmates. It's not about blasphemy, and it's not about presents. I know now that Christmas is a time to be together as a family, and a time to reaffirm our unconditional love for each other. It doesn't have to be with the family you are born into. I have learned you create your family anew and by choice along the way on life's journey.

I still see Christmas through the eyes of that little girl who was bedazzled by the Advent calendar. But now I give her permission to walk through each and every door and to celebrate each day fully and completely. After all, it is a time to dream and believe in the unbelievable.

A young man, head bowed, hands tightly pressed in prayer, knelt on the pavement, oblivious of our bulky broadcasting gear. Another, a tall bearded Parisian, with soft, crinkling eyes, told us in a trembling voice of the sorrow of his eighty-year-old mother, and a daughter of sixteen, over this terrible tragedy. A winsome couple, holding hands in the City of Love, gazed across the River Seine.

We all did.

Everyone and anyone had come to the Quai d'Orleans on this grey overcast day to peer at the scorched Notre-Dame Cathedral of Paris defining the skyline on the other side. On that day, Notre-Dame – Our Lady – seemed truly 'ours'. The blazing inferno which ripped through its roof the night before had also revealed a truth – that this majestic medieval cathedral, sacred to Catholics and Christians alike, also mattered to people of many faiths, and of no faith.

And so too does Christmas.

Ebenezer Scrooge, of Charles Dickens' *A Christmas Carol* fame, would have found it almost impossible to escape this festival in our time. From Juba to Jakarta to Jerusalem, I've seen the same red-coated white-bearded Santas, the same cherubic angels, the same shimmering strings of fairy lights festooning markets and streets. Around the world, in hotels – from one- to five-star – there's usually another glittering star in the lobby, perched on high, on whatever can pass for a Christmas tree.

Sometimes, it amuses. A government office I often call in a predominantly Muslim country in the Middle East has a cheery Christmas carol to listen to while you're on hold, all through the year. Someone must have thought: 'That sounds nice and happy.'

Sometimes, it jars. Elaborate gingerbread houses covered in sweet sugar icing seemed sacrilegious in Syrian hotels during a catastrophic war. Outside, just streets away, entire neighbourhoods were just heaps of rubble, pitch black, in utter ruin.

In 2003, leaving Iraq after covering the discovery of Saddam Hussein in his hideout in a hole in the ground, hotels in neighbouring Kuwait were resplendent with those Santa Clauses who come down a chimney.

And in Thailand, on the first anniversary of what became known as the Boxing Day tsunami, the lights of Yuletide celebrations shared space with candles of remembrance and sorrow to mark the monstrous tide of destruction.

Of course, commercial considerations are often what's fuelling this spread of seasonal cheer across lands of many faiths. In London, with each passing year, the glittering canopies of Christmas lights start going up a little bit earlier around shoppers' central at Oxford Circus. Last year, it even crossed what had always been the little thin line of decency and decorum. They went up before Halloween.

But there must be something more to all this than just marketing and merchandise. For all the differences of our time which pull people apart, something about Christmas now seems to bring us together. As one of the most sacred days in the Christian calendar seeps into other cultures' diaries as a special date, it calls on us to consider just what makes it so powerful for so many around the world.

Growing up in a small city on a little bay in eastern Canada, we were more entranced by Charlie Brown than Charles Dickens. In the annual must-watch cartoon film *Charlie Brown's Christmas*, the wise boy, Linus, described the true meaning of Christmas. It was, he reminded us, perfectly clear in the passage from Luke in the King James Bible, about the birth of Jesus and the angels' celebratory cry – 'Glory to God in the highest, and on earth peace, goodwill toward men'.

Divine glory, and temporal goodness. That seems to sum it up. But, even in 1965, before ubiquitous malls and online shopping, Charlie Brown worried about commercialism crowding out Christianity.

In a city divided between Catholics and Protestants, with a few Jewish families who quietly kept their faith, I found myself poised between one sister who found joy in every ritual from wrapping to ripping open presents, and another who insisted every year that there should be fewer presents, or none at all. But whatever the difference, Christmas loomed large in our big Catholic church-going family. Two grandmothers meant two tables groaning with turkey dinner, with all the trimmings.

But it never ever occurred to me that someone would want to miss it until my first rude awakening at university when some students made it clear they had no interest in going home for this holiday. And when my own travels, post-university, meant I often couldn't go home, I also tried to pretend Christmas didn't exist. That was easier years ago. Flying into Kabul on Christmas Eve in 1988, to the capital of a Muslim country with an embattled Soviet-backed government, there were no Yuletide signs in a harsh winter, in the Cold War.

But, even then and there, a bit of amnesia never worked because something about Christmas is inescapable. And the date is seared in my own diary, partly because my birthday is the day before.

In the 1980s, in a village in Ivory Coast where pagan and Christian beliefs were seamlessly entwined, there was a round yellow pound cake with candles and traditional turkey dinner West African style: bright orange yams and what's known as 'poulet bicyclette', the skinny chicken which races around the yard.

In the 1990s, just before Christmas Eve mass in Bethlehem, in a packed restaurant next to the Church of the Nativity – where Christians believe Jesus was born – every table sang me Happy Birthday in Arabic, English and French.

And now, every year, like most of us, I get greetings from friends the world over, sent digitally, and a diminishing trickle of handwritten cards delivered by a postman or woman to the door. And so, when I turned to the most powerful tool of our time – social media – to find out more about why it matters, friends and fellow travellers posted messages from around the world.

For practising Christians, it's simple: it's about 'the birth of Jesus'. And for those of Orthodox faith, for whom Christmas bells toll a little later, there are two dates to enjoy. Of course, there were some Scrooges with monosyllabic replies: 'never'; 'nope'.

But there was also Ahmad, a Muslim, who wrote of being drawn to the 'love, compassion and humility' of Jesus. Another friend, describing himself as an 'Afghan-born Muslim Australian', called it a 'celebratory time'. Jonathan, a Quaker who believes every day is special and godly, still confessed to liking the songs and mince pies. A Jewish friend Sheila says her family doesn't celebrate the religious side, but enjoys the traditions. Lars, a Norwegian atheist, embraces the pre-Christmas tradition of celebrating midwinter. And Charu, who's Hindu, confessed to putting up mini Christmas trees because 'they look fab'.

But the words 'an excuse' kept appearing – an excuse to get together with friends and family, send cards, share food, feel joy, 'celebrate life'.

At a time of so much distressing news from near and far, in an age when religion is distorted by extremists to divide and destroy, perhaps we all need excuses, and occasions, to savour cherished rituals of faith, family and friendship. And, as our times change, so too do the layers of meaning in an ancient biblical story. A story of displacement, where Mary and Joseph are forced to leave home, and give birth in a strange place in a simple manger now strikes another chord. We can warm to the bright 'Star of Wonder' which guided wise men to them. Then, on the run from authoritarian rule, they become refugees.

Many can see their story in our Christmas story.

Who would not want to see light in dark times? I've even started to think it might be nice if the sparkling Christmas lights of Oxford Circus, just a block away from the BBC, could be up all year round.

That day when many gathered to gaze at a smouldering cathedral on the River Seine was also a day of hope. The fears of the night before, when all seemed lost, had given way to relief that, for all that was gone, so much had been saved. A new and even better Notre-Dame would be reborn. Then, when night fell, a choir suddenly appeared. The strains of a stirring hymn filled a dark sky. People of many faiths, of no faith, all stopped to listen, all finding meaning in a moment of joy.

Maha Thaher

I am Muslim and I celebrate Christmas.

It was never an either/or for me. When people are unified behind core national causes like freedom, and the right to self-determination, and when they face, daily, one of the most protracted conflicts in the world, this unification extends to other parts of the social life, including holidays and celebrations. In Palestine, for the two major religions Islam and Christianity, holidays are celebrated in very similar ways: visiting family and friends, taking part in prayers and worship, eating a lot of sweets and cookies stuffed with dates, and enjoying the holiday decorations and parades. The special traditions and foods of each holiday are long awaited and enjoyed nationally. Whether it is Christians waiting for Ramadan to eat the special sweets called Katayef, or Muslims waiting for Easter eggs; whether it is Christians enjoying the lighting of the Ramadan lantern, or Muslims taking their kids to Christmas parades and the lighting of the Christmas tree. We Palestinians have come to cherish these celebrations, and we view the joy they bring as a part of our culture and a way to celebrate life and the beauty of our diverse society.

I grew up in Palestine. Throughout my childhood, the

Christian faith was a normal part of the social fabric I was in. Many of our family friends and classmates were Christian. I did not know what a predominantly Muslim country meant until I was much older.

Christmas is the cultural event that brings us together, and that helps us, as Palestinians, connect to our roots, the roots of the Holy Land. It is a religious event for those who celebrate it religiously, a cultural one for those who don't. It is a political statement when we defy the checkpoints and roadblocks to reach family or Bethlehem for Christmas Day celebrations.

When my parents divorced, my brothers and I were reaching adulthood and starting to shape our own lives separately from them and our extended family. It was hard for my mother to hang on to us as children, so she kept the Christmas tradition to bring us together as a family every year.

We gather with family on all holidays and important occasions. Yet, the Christmas tree remains a major focus of our small family – we decorate it, cover it in lights, and each of us puts up their own angel: my mother's idea to involve and unite us all. If my father and my mother ever agreed on anything, it was raising us as the creators of our own beliefs and traditions and not to conform to labels or mainstream lifestyles. But celebrating Christmas as a Muslim family and holding it so dear is all down to our mother.

This past Christmas was different. My mother was away doing her Ph.D. and couldn't make it home for Christmas. My brothers and I carried on nevertheless. It took me ages to get the tree out, and ages to convince my brothers to help with the decorations. However, I didn't have to say much when it came to putting up our angels. I laid them out next to the tree and put mine up. One by one, my brothers hung theirs up next to mine. We hung my mother's one too.

My mother arrived on New Year's Eve and we re-hung her angel in a special ceremony. When she went away again, I sat every night next to the tree watching it flicker with all the house lights off. The light, so mesmerising, so soothing, almost like a prayer in itself.

When I set out to write this piece, I thought it would be about deconstructing misconceptions and stereotypes around Christmas, the either/or – are you Muslim or do you celebrate Christmas? I thought it would be about the fact that Christmas is about culture and tradition in the Holy Land, not only about religion, and how can we not celebrate the birth of one of our own? How can this country with its many daily sacrifices not celebrate the one who gave the ultimate sacrifice? And it is, all of this.

When I set out to write about Christmas, I thought that these things are what it meant to me. However, I discovered something beyond all of that, something much more deeply personal. Christmas to me is family. It is home. It is my mother.

MALCOLM WALKER

'I'm on call, but I'll get something in town before coming home, it's always quiet in the holidays and most places are open,' I shouted to my wife as I left the house on the morning of Christmas Eve's eve. It had seemed like such a good idea.

But come the evening after a longer day on the wards than I had anticipated, I am in Selfridges when my bleeper summons me out of the stupor induced by clueless gazing at the offerings on the department store's shelves. Too late, no time to decide, but this interlude won't take long, will it? I'll be back before they close.

The team had gathered already in the Heart Hospital's cath lab as I entered its unnaturally white shadowless light. I noticed the pair of builder's boots, London-clay-stained, sticking out of the paramedic's trolley. There was a busy hustle at the head end, monitor leads, pressure cuffs, the tangle of venous access lines being organised and tidied.

Consent was being obtained. Informed consent? Faced with the given choices: continue having your heart attack, with all that conjured up in the mortally fearful brain, or let us re-open a blocked artery, what's to choose?

'You are having a heart attack. An artery in your heart has

blocked and we need to open it up with a stent, we call the procedure a PCI; but there are some risks attached to doing it . . .'

What does a 5 per cent risk of death or damage mean at this time? The hushed, hurried explanation ran its course and I did not intervene, despite much of me wishing to simplify and take responsibility for the victim – any semblance of choice based on impossibly little information obtained in a crisis. Are we the professionals being self-delusional, assuaging institutional fears and guilt about historical paternalistic approaches to care, rather than being inclusive? At this point in life we crave to be led, be well advised and cared for, don't we?

The decision was made and a scribble applied to a sheet of paper held awkwardly above his chest.

'Collapsed at work, just up the road, no loss of output, no previous, no local next of kin.'

The paramedic, rightfully proud of his work so far, was relaying this to me as I scrubbed and gowned up.

From his collapse to his arrival in the cath lab, it had taken a remarkably short twenty minutes. I looked at him more closely. He couldn't have been more than forty, still with site dust whitening his red hair, slicked by a sweaty forehead, a tiny muddy rivulet coursing in front of his ear.

'Tombstone ST segments on the ECGs, but pressure and sats ok on air.'

It did not take long to manoeuvre the fine plastic catheters, with their cleverly shaped tips, to the origin of the left coronary artery. Muscle memory, an embedded three-dimensional image of the bends and twists of the arterial system, helped me deliver the tubes to their desired position with the minimum of diversions. Injecting an opaque X-ray contrast agent demonstrated the expected sheared-off main coronary artery branch. The LAD. The blockage is known as the 'widow maker' as many operators are fond of informing their charges.

When I first witnessed this conversation, as a cardiology trainee, it struck me as self-congratulatory, disguised as humour, ensuring the clever cardiologist would receive the just quantity of gratitude, not wholly undeserved, but grating to an ingrained self-deprecating near-Englishman. Still, it does provide ammunition to the victim for the pub game of medical and surgical trumps; the quadruple bypass versus the 'widow maker' survivor.

He was in the process of losing the front wall of his ventricle. The catheter-mounted stent and deflated balloon easily crossed the fresh clot blocking the artery. After the first inflation and delivery of the exquisitely crafted metal stent, blood flowed outlining a huge artery. Relief. With this timing the chances were that there would be absolutely no permanent damage to his heart. Brilliant. Truly joyful.

And then: elation, we had finished!

But I still had nothing for the children. And it was now, somehow, one in the morning.

One idea I hatched during a quieter phase of the procedure was the promise of a nice holiday, yet to be booked, in a venue yet to be thought about (and costing so much more than I had hoped to spend).

'Hamleys is open all night tonight,' the cath-lab sister had said, sensing my increasing anxiety.

The virtual holiday now seemed second rate, when compared to the physicality of unwrapping a present, a toy!

The famous toy store was only a short walk away. This was how I found myself the only sober shopper in London's 'emporium of joy'. Perhaps not surprising, given the lateness. I weaved resentfully between unsteady but happy customers and bulging shelves, ducking the mad spitfire as it pursued its tail overhead, furiously circling in an apparent bid for freedom from its tether on the ceiling.

In the end, I did manage to salvage my image, if only to myself, of a 'proper' father. Gifts would be unwrapped. They were all too big, of course, and mostly items that I had craved myself in childhood. But don't all fathers do that to their children?

MEERA SYAL

When I was a kid, I was regularly asked a lot of questions I didn't know the answers to.

'Why do you eat with your fingers?'

'Is your blood red?'

'Do you celebrate Christmas?'

As I got older, the questions became superficially more complex but fundamentally were the same, just dressed up in posher clothes.

'Was your marriage arranged?'

'Would you call yourself an intersectional feminist?'

'Would it offend you if I wore a bindi?'

In fact, all the small questions boiled down to the one big question: Do You Belong? Bit unfair to ask a pre-school British-born kid with recently arrived Indian parents. I suppose we were living in a Black Country mining village where wearing flares was seen as an act of dangerous rebellion.

And what kid doesn't want to belong? I worked hard at that: I had different masks, accents and clothes for Home and Outside. I fluctuated from lilty-Hinglish to a broad Midland drawl in an eyeblink – quick costume change in the wings – head up, speak up, never let the audience smell your fear.

We first-generation kids of immigrants were very good at this bi-cultural shape shifting. We had to be – fitting in meant survival.

But we also had to bring the outside inside and build the bridge between our parents' mother culture and the new one we were forming as we grew up. Some of it was easy: 'Seriously, try the green chillis/garlic/mango pickle with the fish and chips/pizza/Scotch egg – it's so much better . . .' Some of it was less so: 'Everyone else is going down the disco/pub/festival – why can't I?' As I found out, there are lots of shades of compromise, ranging from sunny yellow Yes Go Ahead to angry red Do That And You Will Kill Me With Shame.

Christmas sat somewhere in the middle of the adaptation colour chart for my family. Celebrating it was neither controversial nor a deal breaker, it was a choice. Coming from one of the biggest multi-faith countries in the world, my parents had grown up celebrating everyone's various festivals: Eid, Baisakhi, Janmashtami . . . For them, it was a neighbourly way of saying we respect and appreciate your religion, as I hope you will do mine. For us kids, it was another excuse for lots of food and a party.

Indeed, I attended Sunday School for years at the village Methodist Church, as it was the centre of community social life (so was the pub and the Working Men's Club, but that would have been taking integration a little too far . . .). So I happily sang in the choir, made hats for the Easter Parade and drew lots of pictures of Jesus. My parents didn't mind – they'd always said that all religions led to the same god, or at least the same place where kindness, tolerance and charity meant more than individual ideology.

So while Jesus wasn't our family deity, as the rest of our adopted country were celebrating his birthday big time, my parents felt it would be rude not to join in. My mum, being a primary-school teacher, was entirely plugged into the whole Nativity/carol singing/decking halls with boughs of holly circuit, which in our house translated into one small fake tree overloaded with tinsel cast-offs from her school. Of course our Christmases reflected our dual heritage. The turkey was curried, mince pies sat alongside Indian sweets, post-meal charades was replaced by a Punjabi singalong and my father hurriedly switched television channels during any rude bits in the Bond film.

Then, excitingly, my father announced he would take me to meet the actual Father Christmas at his firm's annual festive bash. I was four years old when I first got to queue up with hundreds of other kids at the magical grotto known as the Willenhall Public Baths. The water had been boarded over, and I was confused that Santa apparently lived above a swimming pool. But he was everything I'd hoped for: fat, white-bearded, smelling of reindeer (this was before I knew what beer smelled like). He gave me a present. He didn't ask what religion I was, how long I'd lived here or whether I ate Christmas dinner with my fingers. This was proof that Christmas was for everybody and that I belonged.

And then I opened the present in the car on the way home. It was a set of plastic witchy fingers, or rather witchy fingertips that fitted on to the end of your fingers, giving you instant talons. Except they were pink. Or 'flesh coloured', as it said on the label. When I wore them, it looked like I'd dipped my little brown hands into icing sugar. Those babies weren't going to fool anyone. If I ever met another witch coming the other way, I was mincemeat.

Strangely, I wasn't surprised. The witchy fingers sat in the same space alongside those people who asked me, with genuine curiosity, 'So do you celebrate Christmas?' As if it were some kind of citizenship exam, an early forerunner of Tory politician Norman Tebbit's 'Cricket Test', who would go on to claim that ex-colonials supporting their native home teams over England's squad was proof that they could never be truly loyal or truly British. But then maybe he'd never tried curried turkey.

My parents put the witchy-finger incident into perspective for me – this was proof that Christmas wasn't about the presents. The real gift of Christmas was that we all got to be together, see friends and neighbours, remember and include those without family or company and enjoy that most precious of gifts – time. And the short version of that was we can't afford XYZ so please don't ask.

Later on, as we became more financially secure, it became about passing that gratitude on. I was encouraged to run errands for elderly neighbours or make a charity donation with my pocket money. Even though we weren't Christian, we could use this as an opportunity to be nicer people. It becomes harder to remember that, when shops start their

Christmas campaigns in October, we now have Black Friday in November and there's nationwide consumer hysteria for most of December. But looking back, what I do remember is not what I was bought, but who I was with, and how lucky I felt to be surrounded with love. That's it really, like all the songs say – that's what anyone really needs. It's free, the more you give the more you get back, it has nothing to do with skin, colour or religion and I'm told it's available all year round. Bargain.

MERVYN BROWN

I was born in 1927 and lived the first ten years of my life in a (then) small North Yorkshire mining village called Liverton Mines. Whenever I think of childhood Christmases, I can't help but again feel those nostalgic surges of unbounded excited anticipation and sheer magic. As a young child of that time, I was not made aware of, and in some ways, shielded from, any of the problems which dogged parenthood, society and the world in general. I now realise, at the ripe old age of ninety-two, just how free I was to enjoy the experiences, explorations and excitement of childhood imaginations: making and putting up the coloured paperchain decorations, the multi-coloured fairy lights and shining tinsel on the decorated tree, the music and carols which filled the air and that aura of goodwill and happiness which, even to a young child, seemed prevalent at that time. How could a child not tingle with the sheer thrill of it all?

And of course, of great importance to come there was Father Christmas.

He was real – because one Christmas Eve on the radio in Children's Hour I heard him talking to 'Uncle Mac' and he said he was just going out to start delivering the presents and if we were good children, he might leave a present at our house. Thus said, Uncle Mac agreed and finished the programme, as he always did in his own quiet way, 'So it's goodnight children . . . everywhere.'

He was real – because his footprints in the soot on the fireplace proved he had come down the chimney.

He was real – because he had drunk the ginger wine and eaten the piece of cake which I had left out for him.

He was real – because when I woke up the following morning, there was the pillowcase which I had hung on my bedpost the night before, full of lovely presents: gold chocolate coins in a small golden net tied with gold ribbon, a white sugar mouse with a tail, a *Rainbow* comic, an orange wrapped in coloured tissue paper, a flashlight whose light you could change from red to green to bright white.

But best of all, there was the present for which I had asked in my letter, ceremoniously sent up the chimney several days before: a Buck Jones Cowboy outfit complete with hat, neckerchief, holster, gun, a roll of caps and a sheriff's badge. Wow! I couldn't wait, so I hurriedly put my costume on, stood in the doorway of Mam and Dad's bedroom and menacingly called out 'Hands up!' The response was so slow I fired two warning shots in the air: 'Csh! . . . Csh . . . !'

I looked out of the window – not an Indian or baddie in sight. After breakfast downstairs at 'The Ranch', I went outside and met some of my friends whom I managed to persuade to go out on to the Common and play Cowboys and Indians. I was both horse and rider as I galloped along with my left arm fully extended in front purporting to hold the reins, and my right hand vigorously slapping my right buttock to make the 'horse' go faster. I could hear the train fast approaching. Would I get there in time to release the girl tied across the lines? (We did have a single-line railway track at the edge of the Common which added a bit of authenticity to our play.)

Such vivid Christmas thoughts do re-ignite the memory and bring to mind those others who were part of the tapestry of both my own and the village life. Mrs Sollitt, for instance, a delightful lady of more mature years who, with full approval of the local doctor, had delivered all the babies in the village (me included). We as children therefore assumed that all you had to do to get a baby was for your mother to put on a clean nightie, go to bed and then send for Mrs Sollitt. Quite a reasonable child logic, don't you think, because we only ever saw Mrs Sollitt go into a house and come out after a while, having just left a baby that hadn't been there when she first went in.

And there was Con (Cornelius) Judson, who to us was a genial, rather elderly character. At one Christmas Carol concert, he was playing his trumpet while accompanying a group of us carol singers. In his attempt to reach a Grand Fortissimo top F finale note for the last verse of 'Hark the Herald Angels', he farted an even more crisp and sonorous note than the achieved top F. Completely unembarrassed by the resultant laughter, Con responded, 'Tell tha what, it nearly made a perfect fifth' (for the benefit of non-musicians a perfect fifth is basically the interval between the first and fifth notes of a major scale).

And also known to all the children and very much appreciated by their parents was Billy Wood, the Bell Man. Such was my friends' and my freedom for play that there were many times our parents didn't know where we were or we hadn't come home for tea. Undaunted and seemingly unperturbed, they would contact Billy who would then walk around the streets, ringing his bell and calling our names. There was always someone who heard him and knew where we were – maybe at a friend's house or playing games on the Common with others. Whatever, we were always located and told to go home.

It also was an era when two or three of us would sing carols outside the doors of selected houses, in the dark but for our flashlight, with the hope of earning a copper or two. On some occasions there would be a friendly response to our gentle seasonal approach.

In complete contrast, some of the kids from Cleveland Street – a virtual no-go area for us children at that time and they could have taught the Artful Dodger a trick or two – would approach strangers or visitors with the rhyme:

> *A hole in mi stocking*
> *A hole in mi shoe*
> *A hole in mi arsehole – just like you.*
> *If you haven't got a penny, a ha-penny will do.*
> *If you haven't got a ha-penny, God bless you.*

Whatever happened to those likely lads, I know not.

I feel that looking back over childhood memories of the past does have a relevant purpose for both the present and the future. As a Christian I am fully aware of and cherish the whole ethos of what Christmas is really about. One of the carols begins, 'Love came down at Christmas'. Let us all keep reminding ourselves of that.

MERYL STREEP

Today, which, like every other day of the year but one, is *not* Christmas, I sit on a couch with my two-week-old grandson snoring on my chest. It is early spring in Los Angeles, which means it is sunny and balmy, like almost every other day in Los Angeles. I put on a recording of Renée Fleming singing 'Silent Night'. The babe relaxes into a sleep deep memory of his infinite pre-birth state, and I reconnect to the meaning of Christmas. A child is born, and it evokes the promise of the ages. This one might save us. This child is our hope.

> *Round yon virgin mother and child*
> *Holy infant, so tender, and mild.*

The circle of care that begins in his mother's womb and carries him into her arms and into the circle of life, will carry him round the days of our turning earth, long after (God willing) we all who welcomed him are gone.

> *Sleep in heavenly peace,*
> *Sleep in heavenly peace.*

The meaning of Christmas has always been about the kindling of hope in dark days, about the promise of peace and the hope that is delivered with the birth of each child. The weight of each child on the chest of our Mother Earth is our responsibility to nurture, care for and celebrate.

It is a gift to be reminded of that by a Christmas lullaby, and not just at Christmas, but on a fragrant spring day as well.

Mike Korzinski

The other day, I asked my sister what she remembers most about Christmas. Her unhesitating answer: 'Ritual humiliation'.

Childhood memories can feel like dreams shrouded in mist that appear in the distance and change shape with time. But sometimes they are a crack of thunder that blasts through the sky. Uncle Hank was that unmistakable crack of thunder. He continues to rumble through Christmas Past but the fury of the storm we once weathered as children has long since blown itself out; mellowed, from our adult perspective, with humour and continuing astonishment that someone could be that mean-spirited and sarcastic on the most hallowed of all days in the Christian calendar (albeit for us hallowed by the candy).

Uncle Hank was married to my Aunt Rita, my father's sister. Every year, they would arrive for Christmas Day lunch, and the ritual would begin. He would greet my grandmother: 'Merry Christmas, Katherine'. Uncle Hank pronounced my grandmother's name in a dulcet descending pitch of contempt and superiority, the spacing of vowels and consonants laced with venom in the form of a smile and pseudo respect. To my grandmother being called by her first name by anyone in the family other than her husband was disrespectful. Doing so risked her ire and Uncle Hank knew it.

'Katherine, would you pass the potatoes please? Thank you, Katherine.' It was relentless. 'Katherine, would you like a drink?' My grandmother did not drink. 'Katherine' was a sledgehammer at the end of every sentence. My grandmother would always be fuming, her glass eye on the verge of popping out of her head. The turkey inevitably suffered the consequences of her rage. It was burnt to a crisp in the all-consuming fire of her oven.

At the height of the Vietnam War it was my father's 'lefty leaning anti-war stance' that became the target. Uncle Hank did not serve in the Second World War. Pop was eighteen when he bore witness to the horrors of Hiroshima and Nagasaki soon after the atomic bombs had been dropped. He remained haunted by the war in ways that took him seventy-five years to understand, and only now at ninety-five does he finally feel a 'bit more free'.

Uncle Hank had a morbid fascination with war films. He spent endless hours watching his war porn in the basement of his house on his big-screen television. In his mind this made him an expert.

Uncle Hank would segue from war into grossly inappropriate remarks imbued with sexual innuendo about my sisters' Christmas dresses. It got worse with every glass of Harveys Bristol Cream. My mother had grown up in a family ravaged by alcohol, feeling abandoned and terrified most of the time, her only refuge her upstairs neighbour who did her best to protect her when the alcohol-fuelled madness that laid siege to her family became too much. This was the nightmare of Christmas Past doing a smash-and-grab raid in the present.

My mom did her best to diffuse and deflect the worst of Uncle Hank's remarks with uncomfortable laughter and futile attempts to redirect the conversation. Her efforts only served to stoke the fires of whatever narrative Uncle Hank was pursuing at that moment. Aunt Rita would giggle: 'Oh, Hank.'

My 'tubby' older brother was not spared. 'Fat' jokes rained down on him. I was too young to remember but my sister says that when – aged six – he first met Uncle Hank he punched him right in the nuts and then ran away. Kids have a way of getting to the point. My brother was always more direct than me and even as a child he had excellent instincts about people.

When I grew up I asked my mom why she didn't ban Uncle Hank. She said in those days it was all about 'family'. If she banished Uncle Hank, it would have severed the connection between my aunt and her parents. My mother would not abandon my aunt; the least she could do was meet for the occasional cup of tea and for Christmas lunch.

Uncle Hank was my godfather. I had no idea what that meant other than if my parents passed away, he was supposed to take care of me. With Uncle Hank looming in the background I prayed hard that my parents did not die (not the only reason!). In the meantime, I did my best to avoid him. I learned to dodge, duck, dive and weave between the onslaughts. Maybe it was because I was unwell as a child and the youngest in a family of people bigger and stronger than me that I learned the importance of movement.

My mother recently told me, 'You danced with Uncle Hank.' I asked her what she meant. 'You matched his steps, move for move. It was something special to watch. No matter what he said, you danced your way through those crazy Christmas dinners at Grandma's house like no one else.'

Uncle Hank's ritual Christmas Day shit thrower spared no one. Nonetheless I choked down my dried-out turkey leg with a singularity of purpose that transported me to a place of pure Christmas bliss. No matter how burnt and dried out the bird, with the right amount of gravy, stuffing and ketchup it was heavenly. Despite Uncle Hank's best efforts, my grandmother's love was baked into every bite.

My brother, sisters and I revelled in each other's company. My grandmother's house was built in the middle of my father's car lot. He was a used-car dealer in New Jersey and would let us drive a three-wheeled mail cart he had purchased so we could learn to drive. We would dash from the dining-room table, keys in hand, each one of us wanting to be first to take a spin. We would joke, laugh, fight and tease one another. Uncle Hank's taunts, from the irritating to the humiliating, receded into the background, drowned out by our laughter as we made the next loop around the dealership car lot.

As we grew older and my grandparents passed away so did the imperative to gather together as a family. My siblings and

I were going our separate ways. No one wanted to face Uncle Hank one on one. As children we were vulnerable but as siblings we had a power that we could not summon up alone.

Was that Uncle Hank's Christmas present to us? Wrapped and packaged with insults and sarcasm, Uncle Hank gifted us with the knowledge that we would survive his Christmas Shitstorm if we stuck together. We were stronger together than when we were alone. We found shelter and joy in each other's company and a bond that Uncle Hank, despite his best efforts, could not break. It was the best Christmas gift ever and one we all value to this day.

Thank you, Uncle Hank. Merry Christmas. Please pass the ketchup.

Mike Tuohy

I started volunteering for Crisis at Christmas forty years ago, in 1979. I was eighteen, and all around me in London I was witnessing a lot of rough sleeping and heavy drinking. I come from an Irish background and I could see that, had my parents gone the wrong way, they might have ended up down that route. At that age, I didn't have a lot of money to give to anyone, but I had time. If you're lucky, you should share the luck.

I remember once chatting to an Irish guy, a heavy drinker, on a cold night in Holborn. I asked him about his drinking and he said, 'Look, tonight I'm cold and wet but tomorrow night is not going to be any better, nor all the nights after that.' Alcohol was taking the edge off things and you could see why he drank. If I was in that situation I probably would have as well. This is why the life expectancy of a homeless person is so low. They don't choose to be homeless.

I met my wife nearly thirty years ago at a Crisis Christmas centre – she was also a volunteer; and I've made great friends there, both homeless guests and volunteers. When we had my son, who's now fifteen, we took him to Crisis because our friends wanted to see our newborn baby. I wear the same kind of shirt every day at Crisis, a lumberjack shirt, which has a teddy bear in the top pocket. It was given to me by one of the guests for my son, when I took him to Crisis to meet her.

The reason we call the homeless people 'guests' at the Christmas centres is because we bring them into our home for that week, and treat them as someone special, when most of the year it's not like that at all for them. Crisis creates an environment where a homeless person can sit down over a cup of tea and have a chat with someone like me as an equal.

It's also a place where they can sleep properly, something they can't do on the streets. Out there, they're always on edge, always looking for the next meal, looking out for who's going to potentially harm them. They sleep well here because they know that someone is looking after them.

They're offered services that are potentially vital steps out of homelessness – fresh clothes, job and housing advice, as well as dentist and pharmacist appointments. And for that one week, we serve them their dinner. It's the only time of year they get served food, because normally they queue up for it. Little things like that are important and they really do appreciate that people are giving up their time on a special day and not being paid.

We've got about 11,000 volunteers and I think they're unbelievable. They go far beyond what someone would ask of them in a normal work environment. I've had volunteers willingly and uncomplainingly clean up after someone's been sick. At the end of the day, we're always there for them.

Many guests walk in hunched up, cold, hungry and frightened. The centres allow our guests to step off the treadmill, sit down and re-evaluate their lives. When they leave, they look taller, smarter and their backs are straighter. They've had a haircut and had their nails cleaned. They feel ready to take on the world again.

Everyone has this preconceived idea that homeless people are all just begging and making a fortune out of it, but if we can get every one of our 11,000 volunteers to go and tell ten of their friends what they are really like, then we're doing a good job because we're spreading the message that they're not how they're portrayed in the press. They are just normal people who but for the grace of God could be any of us, and they just need a bit of help and love.

And that is true all year round, but it's especially true at Christmas.

Nawa Mikhaeil

It would begin like this. A month ahead everyone would be talking about that one very special time of the year: Christmas! Early on 25th, my brother and I would wake up, put on the clothes that we had been waiting to wear for a while, and head to church. It used to be very crowded and as I was very tiny, I was always upset because I could not see the altar due to the tall grown-ups in front of me. That was in the 90s in Baghdad, where of course there was no snow and no Christmas vibes, really.

After church all my family and relatives would gather. The adults would prepare the usual traditional meals: biryani with beans stew, chicken and meat in different dressings. Dishes that used to have great value, because they weren't usually affordable. The atmosphere around the house was joyous and laughter would fill the air.

We, as children, had no care but to try and avoid the grown-ups who would regularly ask us for a glass of water. We would have an amazing time. Of course, we also used to fight and get upset about the silliest matters ever. One year my cousin received Barbie dolls which she got as a gift from relatives in Germany. From that day on I remember I cried every time we had to leave their house, because I was heading out without the pretty dolls.

Now, when we gather at Christmas, all of my little cousins are playing on their phones and tablets. The scene entertains me while remembering how it was when I was their age. Whenever I think that what they are doing is wrong, they prove me wrong by saying very smart things (learned from their phones and tablets). Therefore, I just enjoy watching them feeling content in their own little world.

During my adolescent life, living in Sulaimaniyah city in Iraq, a party only for Christians would be held on the second day after Christmas. It was always a challenge to convince my brother to come to this party with us, and more challenging was convincing him to dance with me. In the Chaldean community in Iraq, it is not common for girls and boys to dance together unless they are relatives, engaged or married.

Therefore, I did not really enjoy those parties and all they made me feel was tired! But I have to admit, I kind of enjoyed seeing people happy, the vibes were very positive and love was in the air. Also, it was good to be back to my culture for a few hours and see how the people of our community were carrying out their lives.

When I reached the age of twenty-six, I changed and challenged many things in my life. As a female in a Middle Eastern society, it was difficult to convince those around me that I could do the things in life that are not expected of ladies. There was always that part of me that was ready for the next fight, because I never fancied what was easy and traditional. On the contrary, I always aimed for what was semi-impossible.

I started working and going to college the same week. It was all too much to do together, but I loved the stress and the taste of achievement. Ever since, I have been in different jobs, one better than the last, and thus I continued. I had to fight for my latest job, because I had to move to Erbil city for it, which was a big no for my family, but in the end they supported my decision.

I was there last Christmas – a very different and lonely one. It was the first Christmas I had without going to church on the 24th. There were no tiring commitments, just me alone at home watching the television programme *Friends*. On Christmas morning I woke up and decided to go to a nearby church as I lived in the famous Christian district, Ainkawa. As I walked around the alleys and the neighbourhoods, I saw big families getting out of their cars, obviously gathering at the grandparents' house. Many others were rushing to the grocery stores for last-minute purchases, and I observed many neatly dressed men visiting their neighbours one after the other to wish them merry Christmas and catch up on news, which is a tradition in our country (since we do not exchange gifts at Christmas, it does make it easier), and noted the smell of good food mingling with the fresh morning air. By the time I arrived at church, the mass was over and I was told to return the day after.

Reflecting while retiring to bed that night, I realised how the bond is strong between such events and family. It is inevitable to feel emotional and nostalgic for home. Thinking about starting a family was also inevitable, as if I had an epiphany. It also reminded me that there is war and violence in other cities of my country, and so many people do not have what I have. It pained me how life can be cruel for some. I counted my blessings and wished that one day those people will taste the peace and freedom I was feeling in that moment.

NI NI MYINT

Living in a country where only about 6 per cent of the population are believed to be Christians, Christmas was not a very popular festival in Myanmar (formerly Burma). The beginning of Christianity in Myanmar dates back to the arrival of Portuguese missionaries in 1554, and was latterly carried on by British and American Baptists. Until our independence from the British in 1948, it was allowed to preach and talk about the gospel, but from 1962 onwards, when the military took over, Buddhism was made the de facto state religion and Christianity was portrayed as the 'foreign religion'.

Christian persecution became rife. I grew up hearing about missionaries and pastors being put in prison, I saw Bibles being burnt and churches closed down. I had never witnessed a big celebration of Christmas until 2017, when the government began to celebrate it officially, and of course now it is commercialised for business purposes.

I belong to the Chin ethnic group in Myanmar who were animists by origin. My grandmother was among the first to convert to Christianity in the 1920s. I remember her telling me that they were chased out by the villagers because of their belief. I am very proud to have been born into the first convert family in Chin Hill.

Chin State is the poorest state in my country. I grew up hearing that for the poor people, Christmas is the only time of the year that they eat meat. It sounded funny but that's the reality of where I came from. My childhood Christmas memories were all about getting new lace dresses, feeling like a princess and feasting in the church. But when my dad's business wasn't doing well and new clothes were not possible, my mum would take us to the big sales areas, filled with heaps of used clothes to try and find a suitable dress. I think often these hand-me-downs were even more beautiful than the new Christmas clothes that my friends were wearing. It is just now that I realise that Christmas was already teaching me where contentment lies.

I guess the meaning of Christmas changes as we grow old. In 2006, Dad's business was broken up and we ended up having a lot of debts and not even a handful of rice to eat as a family. But as we pray, the Lord provides. We didn't have a fancy car and new clothes, but we had each other, and that year Christmas was all about 'one day at a time' and that God is faithful in his promises but in his own time.

In 2013 and 2015, when my elder brother and my father who were the breadwinners of the family went to be with the Lord, our Christmases were not easy. As God reminds us that he is in charge of us and we should just believe in him.

It is easier to suffer alone, but when your family are suffering along with you, you groan in pain and it was very hard to find the meaning in Christmas and to talk about why Jesus came. As the hymn says, 'We'll understand it better by and by', and it is true.

Yes, the meaning of Christmas might change based on the situation we are in, but it is always true for me that Christmas is all about home and family. You could be anywhere, in any country, but Christmas means you are going home.

Entering into the world of humanitarian and development sectors fighting for justice and peace, I realise the meaning of Christmas also stands for hope and freedom. And it no longer centres around myself but others, and the people I am working with. Christmas symbolically illustrates Jesus becoming human as a peacemaker, wonderful counsellor and freeing us from the bondage of sin. But what about from the bondage of oppression, injustice, inequality and discrimination in the real world that we live in?

It is very difficult to find a meaning in Christmas when the Rohingya women groups that I work with in the Rakhine State of Myanmar say, 'Every morning the children wake up and ask for food, but what can we give when we don't regularly eat two meals a day?' What does Christmas mean when you have been living in a camp your whole life? What does hope mean for the people who are not hearing Christmas carols but the sounds of guns and bombs, and every day is purely about survival? What does home and family mean when your house was burnt down and when you saw your parents and siblings shot dead in front of your eyes? What does freedom mean when your movement is restricted even in a place where you are citizen?

I have been trying very hard to find the meaning and to make Christmas relevant and comforting, but when living in the real world, those fancy religious words sometimes are more irritating than comforting.

I guess I don't have the right answer and maybe I don't have to answer.

Life can be challenging. You may find yourself sleeping alone on a minus-four winter night without proper blankets and struggling more with the coldness in your heart than the coldness outside. But the purpose of Christmas was Jesus becoming one of us, human. That humanness of God that passed through all the suffering, his victory at the cross and resurrection gave us a glimpse of hope. That one day, everything will be over and maybe we will have the courage to say, 'This too shall pass.' I don't know when I will ever see that peace prevail in my country, where people will learn how to coexist or be tolerant of each other. I don't know when I will be treated equally despite my ethnicity and religion.

Will I ever see that change in my lifetime? I don't know and I don't have the answer. But my hopes and prayers will always be there while I live on this earth.

OLIVIA COLMAN

I get genuinely excited about Christmas. Our youngest still believes in the magic and that makes it so special. But, beyond that, I love a jumper, I love food, I love being with as many people that I love as possible.

Despite trying to curb the presents (we buy three per child), when you add grandparents, godparents, friends and relations, it becomes a little obscene. You can see the impact of each carefully chosen gift diminishing with each new shower of coloured paper. I understand that when we talk about 'the magic' of Christmas for younger children, we do partly mean the magic of this twinkly, elf-borne bounty appearing out of nowhere. But I hate that it can sometimes feel like it's about the sheer quantity of presents. Really, the magic is about goodness, isn't it? Sheer, unadorned (and unexplained) goodness, coming out of nowhere. If I had my way, it would work like this . . .

One handmade present each (if you really want the heated socks, maybe you can get them for your birthday?), something possibly a bit shit, but thought about, maybe wobbly, but made by the hand of someone.

Then, I wish it was about really checking everyone you

live near is ok. Everyone cooking an extra dish, taking it to the family that might really appreciate it, inviting in the old neighbour who's on their own. Everyone buying a seat at the Crisis Christmas table!!! Everyone checking what's needed at the local food bank.

I don't know. I know I often wish more would happen to show warmth to others. And I won't claim I'm an angel myself in that regard – it's so easy to lose track of your own good intentions when Christmas is bearing down on you. But I do think we're forgetting what Christmas is. And there are still wonderful selfless people who do all those wonderful things. How do we make it a thing that we ALL naturally do at Christmas? And every other week in between?

PAUL FEIG

Christmas always fucked me up.

As a kid growing up in Michigan, I looked forward to it so much that it overtook my brain for two months at the end of each year. I would spend all my time thinking about what gifts I wanted, about how I was going to get two glorious weeks away from school and about all the amazing food and desserts I was going to be allowed to eat in a household that normally forbade me from eating sweets.

My anticipation for the holiday was so all-encompassing and extreme that by the time it was over and New Year's Day was upon me, I would be thrown into such depression, such let-down, such despondency at the fact that another Christmas was behind me that my return to school and normal life felt like heading into the gulag for a ten-month sentence.

In the midst of all this was Christmas Day itself. With all the psychotic pressure I put upon this twenty-four-hour period, which I was told in Sunday school apparently celebrated the Birth of Christ, the day itself was always perfect in my book. Up at the crack of dawn to run out and find a mountain of presents (because I was an only child and so what other kid did they have to buy gifts for?) and then watch my mom and dad kiss when Dad gave Mom a piece of jewellery (the only time I'd see them exchange any sign of affection all year), then off to my favourite cousins' house on a cool island called Grosse Ile in the middle of the Detroit River, then a huge turkey lunch that my aunt who was a great cook would make with the best mashed potatoes I'd ever had in my life, then an enormous pile of presents stacked in the middle of my aunt and uncle's living room that we'd hold hands and march around singing 'Here we go 'round the Christmas tree on a cold and frosty morning, there's something for . . .' and then they'd say my name and I'd open one of the numerous presents that they had bought for me, then eat leftover turkey sandwiches in the evening and take the long ride home, drunk on the spirit of family, greed and overconsumption.

It was glorious.

But then it was over for another year, with only my birthday in September as a distant consolation prize.

When I got older and moved to Los Angeles to get into show business, Christmas became more of a quest to try and recapture the fun Yuletide joys of my youth. It never went well. The very first Christmas I spent away from Michigan and my parents saw me going to the family home of a comedy-club waitress friend I was in love with, thinking it would result in romance. But it only resulted in her leaving early to meet a boyfriend I didn't know she had and me going to the movies by myself. Gone were the presents and the homemade food and the fun and the love.

The subsequent years found me becoming more and

more cynical about Christmas and convincing myself that it was just a dumb commercial holiday whose customs were rooted in paganism and so everyone who tried to make it into some big religious holiday was a hypocrite/lemming/rube/intellectual inferior and all the other snarky things we think of other people when we're trying to be cool and smart in our twenties.

The spirit of my materialistic Christmases had died in me.

Ironically, I went on to make two Christmas movies in my career. The first one was a hugely unsuccessful 2006 film called *Unaccompanied Minors*, about a group of kids who get stranded in a snowed-in airport on Christmas Eve and bring holiday joy to all the other stranded passengers. And the second one is *Last Christmas*, which I just made with the wonderful Emma Thompson (perhaps you've heard of her). The reason I bring this up is that I've now had in my life two separate experiences in which I lived and breathed nothing but Christmas for twelve straight months in a row. In pre-production, in production and in post-production, all I thought about, all I looked at, all I heard was Christmas. The colours, the lights, the songs, the decorations, the message of love and goodwill were my 24/7 companions.

Enough to drive any Christmas cynic crazy, right?

Well, here's the thing. It didn't drive me crazy. It made me happy. I looked forward to every day of it. I loved finding the right music and seeing the fairy lights and the falling snow. But I especially loved feeling the spirit of Christmas every day of the year. And while I know that the material elements of Christmas were buoying me, it was something more than that, a realisation.

Christmas shouldn't be a one-day-a-year thing. The feelings of happiness, of goodwill, of charity, of forgiveness and healing, of family and warmth and love of our fellow humans, those are things we should be feeling every day. We should be keeping that alive in ourselves and in the people around us.

The spirit of Christmas should be like the nice people at those water stations that keep runners going during a marathon. There's always someone there handing them sustenance, giving them encouragement, celebrating their accomplishment of pressing forward and doing good. The spirit of Christmas should do that for us during the marathon that is each year, and we in turn should be providing that same service for our fellow runners in this race called 'life'. The Christmas spirit can keep us all moving forward and doing the right thing as we go through each day.

So, let's free Christmas from its one-day-a-year confines and let it become our life coach, our supporter, our motivator and our loving friend. We're only wasting it to do otherwise.

Phyllida Law

My son-in-law has asked me to write a piece about Christmas. Well, I'm not doing anything about the baby Jesus.

I'll start with the turkey. It was gigantic. My mother won it in a local raffle. To protect it from dust from our coal bin, we hung it high up and tied it firmly to the kitchen pulley, which was decorated in items of old underwear. Daisy the dog was entranced, so we shut her in the china cupboard and went to bed. Creeping out of bed to steal chocolate buttons, we found the kitchen was bathed in a green phosphorescent light. It was the turkey. I don't know who it was who freed Daisy the dog from her restraints, but she reasonably started on a drumstick.

I remember my mother scrubbing the wound and stitching the turkey's leg back into position.

We ate it all. It was delicious.

Mincemeat had to be left out on the kitchen table for everyone to stir and add something over the weeks leading up to Christmas. We'd wrap threepenny bits and sixpences in greaseproof paper with a twist, and drop them in.

Father was in an aeroplane somewhere, avoiding Germans. He was never there really. He walked too fast for me when he was around, I couldn't keep up. He sometimes bought me homemade toffee at the Glasgow Botanical Gardens. I never thought it was good enough. I don't remember his presence at all at Christmas time.

We always gave the coal man a present, and the man who lit the gas lamps.

Christmas meant you went home.

I was an evacuee.

One year, Uncle John took us away for a Christmas holiday in a hotel in Largs (a wee town outside Glasgow), on the Clyde.

We needed a furniture van to get us all to the station.

I remember Grannie sitting on a huge wicker skip.

I loved Largs because you could get a bag of hard-boiled sweets called Soor Plooms (for those not up on the Scottish vernacular: Sour Plums . . .) at the local café.

There was a huge two-storey Christmas tree in the hotel lobby, beautifully decorated, and our parcels were all scattered underneath it.

When it came to opening them, I got a tea set – a beautiful one with matching milk jug, sugar bowl and tea cosy.

Everybody seemed thrilled with what they'd received, but I cried because I didn't want the tea set. I hid underneath the table sobbing, inconsolable, because what I really wanted was the dolly that was at the top of that enormous tree. I was painfully in love with her.

The dolly was in a little gingham frock and an apron.

She was black.

This is 1942.

Despite what many believe, Christmas is still celebrated in Ipswich, often annually, in much the same fashion as it is in the developed world.

People are cheery and full of the futility of hope. Lights start to go up around the place in September, and they will stay there till the clocks go forward. Often people can afford to illuminate these lights but will save money by having them blink on and off. People often travel to Ipswich just to see the Christmas lights, unless they live closer to any other town.

But what did Christmas mean for me? As an Ipswichian, I was grateful for what I had: easy access to reasonably priced, non-branded footwear, very few hills and a sense that any smugness about one's circumstances was inappropriate.

Christmas also meant an increase in my domestic work-load. I would assist my mother (a Norwegian whose principal adversary was dust) in decorating the whole house, and while doing so, she would assist me in my understanding that without protracted preparation, there can be no spontaneous fun. Before any decorating, we would give the house a Thorough Clean. The house would already be clean enough to use as an operating theatre, but the suspicion remained that there might be dirt hiding beneath all that sterilised gloss. After the Thorough Clean:

1. All surfaces were covered in season-specific tablecloths.

2. The bannister would be wrapped in tinsel.

3. All door frames would be outlined in tinsel.

4. The cupboards would be used to store replacement tinsel.

5. Bowls of nuts would appear, gathering together once more the uneaten nuts from previous Christmases. No living creature could open these nuts. They were so old that they were, by any reasonable assessment, fossils.

6. The Christmas tree, purchased in mid-November to beat the rush, was placed in (what I still contend was) a too-small flowerpot and kept in precarious place with impacted, wet newspaper; a melange which, by the end of the holiday, would concretise into a giant pine-strewn ring.

7. Christmas Biscuits were baked. These were like normal biscuits, but it was Christmas. Hence 'Christmas Biscuits'. You know, like 'Christmas Meat'. There was a coconut biscuit, a chocolate biscuit, a ginger biscuit and a 'white' biscuit (composition unknown). I would say that over the Christmas period, I would eat between two and three hundred Christmas Biscuits. Each genus of Christmas Biscuit was stored in a large Tupperware box, and the many layers of Christmas Biscuits were separated out with kitchen roll. The kitchen roll showed a festive tableau of Christmassy good-will, but the grease from the biscuits would soak into the

paper, giving the scenes a somewhat sullied feel; a literal blot on the season.

8. Christmas Meringues were made. I would probably eat between eight and twelve Christmas Meringues a day. At no point did my mum try to stop me from eating Christmas Biscuits or Christmas Meringues. If I ever finished a plate of Christmas Biscuits, she would just bring me another plate of Christmas Biscuits. If I started to feel sick from all the Christmas Meringues, she would just tell me to 'take a break', the implication being that I would obviously keep eating Christmas Meringues, I just had to rest. Often she would wake me up in the morning with a plate of Christmas Biscuits or, if I was looking bloated, a couple of Christmas Meringues.

Throughout Christmas, I slept like a cobra, curled up, trying to break down the glucose. Even now, if I open a box of donuts, I have to tell myself not to eat all twelve.

My dad (a Nigerian whose principal adversary was levity) did not eat Christmas Biscuits/Christmas Meringues because he didn't like 'sweet stuff'. His favourite food was raw onion. I would frequently have to bring him raw onion slices as a snack, which meant I began to associate my dad's hunger with crying. I looked forward to reaching a similar state of zen, wherein I too could view my lethal breath as Other People's Problem. 'Who am I trying to impress?' he would say. Yet, ironically, his steadfast refusal to try to impress was impressive.

After the Thorough Clean, it was really just about counting down the days. There were three of us, and as far as my dad was concerned, Christmas just meant he had to eat two, possibly three meals wearing a paper hat. The rest was literal gravy. Norwegians have their main meal on Christmas Eve – roast Norwegian pork, boiled Norwegian cod and Norwegian sauerkraut (*surkål*). We were no different, except for the boiled cod, because my mum always felt cod was 'too fishy', i.e. too ontologically itself. Instead, we would have a Nigerian side dish (something made from beans that had been soaking since the introduction of the decimal system and then cooked in tin foil). My dad would cover this with dried, crushed chilli peppers. Whenever I see 'fusion' food, I wonder whether anyone would dare combine what was combined in our house. Our food was beyond fusion; it was a dialectic.

Norwegians exchange gifts on Christmas Eve. I felt this was both a ruse to prevent me getting up early on Christmas morning and a way to blackmail me into a flurry of chores. My mother dismissed this as another of my deranged paranoiac fantasies, like how it was safe to go outside after 5 p.m. After the last of the sauerkraut had been washed down with a quenching draught of *julebrus*, we would clear the table, wipe the table, dry the table, replace the tablecloth, wipe the tablecloth, dry the tablecloth, wash the dishes, dry the dishes, put away the dishes in the cupboard, wipe the cupboard, dry the cupboard, vacuum any dust resulting from opening the cupboard, wipe the vacuum cleaner, put away the vacuum cleaner in another cupboard, wipe down and dry that cupboard, shower, dry ourselves, wash the towels, dry the towels and sit down on the freshly wiped sofa to exchange tokens of esteem. When I say 'we', I mean my mum and I. By this time, my dad would be asleep.

My mother always felt guilty that our family was so small. But I was happy. The thought of clearing up after another person was too terrifying to contemplate. Regardless, my mother would make sure that some of the presents I received would be 'from' our pets, so that it felt like I was part of a wider community. As a result, I never believed in Father Christmas, but I did believe that my pet rabbit went shopping.

But of all my Christmas Memories, my most enduring is of a strange ornament that would hang from the architrave of the kitchen door. It was a mini-snowman (standard features: big belly, carrot nose, top hat, pipe), but below his bottom section/anus* dangled some foliage which – only now – I realise was mistletoe. I simply thought this snowman's somewhat greenish poo had frozen on exit.

But the main reason I loved this snowman was because of something else below its snowbottom: a metal chime hung within the mistletoe, and it tinkled beautifully when you touched the foliage. When I was a small child, I lacked the height to reach it, but I would hear it sound every time my mother went in and out of the kitchen to bake more Christmas Biscuits. And if she had to pop to the shops, or if she was

---

* What do you call the lower portion of a snowman? They don't have legs ordinarily, so is the anus underneath? Are we dealing with a being that's essentially all torso? Or are the legs implied, which would place the anus in the middle of the back?

out at work, I would draw up a chair, stand on my tiptoes and tinkle the chimes on my own. If anybody else had been there, if there had been any witnesses, they would have seen a small boy stretching upwards, to the limits of his capacity, as if to summon somebody, anybody, to hold him close.

Is Donna Jensen really so different from that little child?

Rose Nam

The Christmas carols had been playing for a whole month in the shops on the high street. I kept expecting to get into the spirit. Finally, it was Christmas morning and I realised the spirit just wasn't coming. Sitting here in my room, it would be just another ordinary day if I wasn't feeling so sad and lonely. Because I will be alone at Christmas for the first time. I can't help but imagine how things would have been if I were still home.

My cousins would have arrived around mid-December, bringing with them live chickens and goats from my aunties and uncles. I would have been planning to make my trips to the villages to deliver goodies for loved ones. The Christmas spirit would increase each day, building to a crescendo on the 24th.

We would stay up very late preparing all types of dishes, but most importantly meat, since between the 23rd and the 26th we would slaughter the birds and animals, eat all the meat we desired and on Christmas Day we would even drink soda for good measure; this was the only time of the year when these foods would be available in plenty! We would dress up the Christmas tree with whatever decorations we could find and even though there would be no presents under it, we took pride in it.

On Christmas morning, we would put on our best clothes and happily walk the mile or so to church, calling out to one and all along the way – 'Hello, merry Christmas!' – before congratulating them on celebrating yet another Christmas. The church would literally overflow with all and sundry. The church service would be three hours long, then once we exited church, we would spend some time meeting and greeting folks we hadn't seen in a year; either because they had moved away and were only back for the Christmas festivities or simply because they were only Christmas churchgoers. No matter, we would all be excited like kids. There was no way anybody would make one angry on this day; not even the village drunk who would juxtapose his own words into the Christmas carols. Much as it was a celebration of the birth of Jesus Christ, we celebrated family togetherness, with food and dance and drinks and a lot of love.

Back home, we would swap funny stories of Christmases past and we would laugh until our ribs hurt while we ate and drank (usually talking during meals was unacceptable, Christmas was an exception). Since we would be seated under the biggest tree in the compound, we would invite whoever would be passing by to come and join the festivities.

I am now here in England, so I say to myself:

'Come on, young lady! Get on with your life! You cannot live in your past, you are in England, a land of plenty. Listen to the sounds of Christmas songs everywhere! Beautiful! Streets lit with decorations. Amazing!'

But sombre thoughts and a feeling of guilt linger at the back of my mind.

'You are alone. Your son is not here. How can you feel good? What is your son going to wear? What is he going to eat? He misses you! Who is he going to be with? Friends or family? Do his mates not have their mothers around either?'

It's yet another day at work, and all the teams are talking about forthcoming Christmas parties. I try to keep myself busy with work, lest I get distracted with my thoughts about the whole Christmas thing.

Then, boom! A colleague asks, 'So what are you doing for Christmas? Anything exciting?' I think for a minute, and then feel it is ok for me to let it out. I open up and tell her how I cannot wait for Christmas to come and go.

'I will attend the night carols at a nearby church on Christmas Eve and spend Christmas Day alone. I'll probably spend it doing my assignment. Oh, actually, my vicar invited me for lunch. She will be cooking for the homeless and she would like me to join them.'

She seems to feel sorry for me, and she tells me I am more than welcome to join her family. I feel so excited for a minute, as I would experience the English way of celebrating Christmas. But as I walk home from work, my thoughts wander again. 'Hang on, I do not drive and there will not be public transport on the day. How do I get to her place?' Thoughts of Christmas being a family day return, I drown in sorrow and tears begin to roll down my cheeks. I think to myself, 'In future, perhaps I should arrange something for people like me to spend the festive period together.' Then I remember my favourite Christian hymn and begin to sing to myself as I walk:

The God of love my shepherd is, and he that doth me feed;
while he is mine and I am his, what can I want or need?
Or if I stray, he doth convert, and bring my mind in frame, and
all this not for my desert, but for his holy name.

And finally, alas! It's Christmas morning. I can't be bothered to get out of bed and I am amazed how calm I feel; not really bothered about being alone. 'It's just another day,' I say to myself. I manage to drag myself out of bed and make a cup of tea, wondering what I should prepare for lunch. Then I feel I can't summon up the energy at the moment and go back to bed.

I play some music on my phone, and begin to think about my assignment. So I get out of bed and realise it is 13:30! Then I hear a knock on my door. Oh my God! It is the vicar! 'We are ready and only waiting for you,' she says. No chance of escaping! I apologise and tell her I shall join them in fifteen minutes.

I get to the church and the table is laid. Everyone welcomes me. I feel at ease and tuck into the delicious assortment of dishes; some of them African, prepared by volunteers. We all have fun and the vicar encourages everyone to take 'doggy bags' to avoid wasting the food.

I stroll back to my flat, call my son to find out how the day went and thank God it is all over!

RUPERT FRIEND

There is a family home in New York City, near the famous comedy club in Greenwich Village and close to a restaurant that serves the most expensive burger you've ever had, and probably the best, unless you have a love of dirt burgers from dive bars, which let's face it, most of us do. An unassuming door is often repainted due to its having once been Bob Dylan's door, and myriad New York visitors feel the need to Sharpie their names on it to (presumably) ally themselves with their folk hero. A sentiment which the current owners of the door understand but do not endorse, hence the ever-present smell of fresh paint.

If you are a waif or a stray, or a ne'er-do-well, or someone who is far from their family, or perhaps has brought their loved ones with them but in so doing has declared that 'family' is a chosen term not to do with bricks and mortar, you'll ring the bell.

You are welcomed with a kiss on both cheeks and with bowls of candied orange peel and shelled walnuts. There is a real fire burning in the grate.

As you move into the main room a spectacle dominates. A *presepio* – the Nativity scene – fills a corner. Scrunched blue paper balls form the sky; real moss on real rocks represent the land. A glass waterfall tumbles into a pool where water is collected in amphorae and taken to bakeries where three-inch bakers turn it into bread which three-inch drunkards eat while they squall and bicker with same-sized farmers and all and sundry ignore the pariah taking an eighth-sized shit in the corner of the scene.

You take in this frozen moment in time and realise it breathes and moves more than any motion picture. Each figure carved to have personality and life, and each placed such that their world is not only legible but in motion.

Each year this tableau will be different; you cannot take it for granted. Each year you must search out The Shitty Man and understand why he snuck off, from whom and what he ate twelve hours prior.

You'll take a glass of something, and perhaps another unsalted nut. You'll look about yourself and realise that there are people here from all over. The phrase 'Christmas is a time for families to get together' will flicker in front of your mind, and you will find it right and true.

A gong will sound. All parties will move to the long table, the one made up of all the tables the apartment has, assembled together and covered in crêpe paper. Neapolitan bingo cards will be handed out, and scores of dried red beans too; these last to serve as counters. The traditional game of 'Tombola' will begin, a bingo-esque endeavour wherein numbers are called which correspond to their (ancient Neapolitan) double-entendre ('The Eye That Looks Down': cunt. 'The Squid and the Guitar': sexual intercourse). You place a bean on the number if you have it; two, three, four or five numbers in a row correspond to a prize. Dollar bills are divided into prize piles for each stage of winning; the double-edged prize being the award for covering your entire card with beans, on which 'Tombola!' is shouted out. While affording the largest cash reward, completing Tombola comes with the requirement that the winner sing a song 'from their own country or tradition' or forfeit the prize. Many a canny Tombola player has been known to misplace a bean here and there and so avoid this lucrative exposure.

The tired fathers drink as much wine as they can during the game's distraction, and the more tired mothers relish the countless willing aunties and uncles who take a turn dandling the little ones so that their mothers may talk of something other than walking and talking and schooling. It is, however, not too long before all are yawning and stretching and reaching for coats and scarves and pushchairs.

The hardened few who remain wait with held breath for the door to swing shut for the final time. And then out comes the Real Game. *Sette e mezzo*, or 'seven and a half', is the game Neapolitans play once the Tombola players have gone to bed. Oversized tarot cards, scaled to suit a giant's hand, display Neapolitan princes, kings and sceptres. Akin to blackjack, the dealer asks each player to look at the card he has been dealt and place real money on top of it. In all likelihood this is the money just won at Tombola: it is a debatable truism that the kings and queens of Tombola are so crowned because they have succeeded in a game of chance, and feel that they must now test their ill-gotten winnings in a game that asks more of them.

The dealer – usually your gracious and twinkling host – asks that you risk whether you or he will end the round with a total score closer to seven and a half, and pays out based on the outcome of same. The cards are painted beautifully, although the numerical value of each is sometimes difficult to decipher: warranting a surreptitious conference with a bankrupt (and hence unthreatening) neighbour to help determine its value.

One card reigns above all: the 'Jolly'. A prince with a golden sun up and to his right, this card can be whatever you want him to be. If you are unsure as to whether you truly hold this card, or merely a similar counterfeit, you may do well to play 'as if', for many a dealer has broken his own bank believing that his opponent held a card that he merely imagined he had.

As the various waifs and strays come to the end of another Christmas they have chosen to share with one another, there is a bittersweet feeling in the air. They hope that they will see one another again in this place, at this time next year; most know that the nature of what they do will guarantee it will not be before then.

SADIE HASLER

I thought Christmas was dead. A corpse that despite its very definite persisting flatline got dragged out of the crypt every year for a bit of poking and titivation by necrophiliac lunatics.

'You sick bastards,' I'd think, staring at families happily piling boxes of orange Matchmakers into their trolleys.

But there is no escaping Christmas. Not in this world.

Christmas died two deaths for me. But I forgot the first for a while because the second squashed it so completely. A tea party trampled by the Rio carnival.

The first I spent waiting for my father to tell us he was dying. 1998. My first year of university. That summer he'd told Mum he had six months to live and she'd lumbered that around a while in dread, before preparing us for the worst. Except she didn't know what the worst was because he hadn't told her how or why he was dying. He wouldn't. She'd asked, repeatedly, for months. Then at Christmas he invited my sister and me to stay with him in Wales. Mum said it was so he could tell us that, next year, he would not be here. We boarded a train knowing that and arrived in a Welsh town knowing that and sat on our beds with our bags knowing that and waited.

But he didn't say anything. We had a Christmas of sorts. And then we left. Nothing was ever said about it again.

That was the first.

The second one trounced it. This time, five years later in 2003, my father decided to really ramp it up a bit by committing suicide/killing/hanging/topping himself/kicking the bucket/taking his own life. (I never know which one to use; it's like having too many nice dresses.) It was the opposite of not dying, death-wise. It was October, which gave us a real chance of letting it sink in in time for Christmas. Fa la la la la, la la la la. In calendar terms, it's when the supermarkets bring out the orange Matchmakers at the same time as the trick-or-treat shit. His death fell in with all that.

Christmas was over. Joy obliterated.

The next year came the Boxing Day tsunami, and beleaguered and broken I watched the footage on the television and wanted to die beneath those waves. I wanted to be dragged along and pummelled and stretched and ripped by trees and rocks and cars and houses, until there was no life left in me. It seemed more honest. Nature's display of strength a kindness; taking away some of the dreadful choice us humans are endowed and burdened by. What was the point? Christmas was dead. I wanted to die.

But so much of life has to be lived for others. It's not just yours. Having lost Dad to suicide I was painfully aware of this. And so Christmas became a macabre dance. I could be pouring wine into people's glasses, even laughing at someone's joke, but in my mind I was resting a paper hat on Dad's head, that funeral-home dead-body version of him lying permanently in state for moments of ceremonial visitation. Unbidden sick imaginings at the dinner table while Dean Martin crooned his best.

He was always there.

(Dad. Not Dean Martin.)

Funnily, I always associated Christmas with the wonder Dad brought to it. The fun and magic. He was great at Christmas. He was jolly and entertaining and wonderful at buying presents that felt like totems of potential. He didn't just give gifts, he gave a new slice of the world for you to eat.

So, from the first shimmer of tinsel, ever earlier in the year, to the smashing of the last bauble and the defenestration of the tree, I learned how to go through the motions. I felt an echo of a drum that used to make me dance. I felt the muscle memory of it flexing in me. But I felt no hope of ever feeling joy.

And then, Time. Time works its magic. Time really does work.

Sixteen years after the second death of Christmas, the year my Dad actually died instead of the year he just said he was going to die, I feel joy again.

I have a daughter now.

My daughter, Marcie, who is one, throws her head back and laughs and freezes in a grin so wide, and what compounds the magic with a ferocity that makes my heart vomit, is I know she is doing it partly for me. She wants to make me laugh; she has learned that trick. She has already entered the game of living for others. I worry she sees a sadness and feels it her job to ease. But that is just me, seeing things from my side. She is a new thing. She has all her Christmases to come. And that returns me to the happiness of my Christmases as a child, almost as though the years of pain in between have been blurred with a fog. Time.

I think about how I will tell her about my father, about how great he was at so many things. How she would have liked him. Loved him. I think about how one day, much later, I will have to tell her how he died. About how some people get so sad they can't imagine a time they don't feel sad anymore. I imagine her face, a future face I don't know yet, processing this. It's too much.

But then.

There is a then.

There is a when and a next and a now, and it's her not him, and it's life and it's joy and it's hope.

I want her to feel the dancing lunacy of Christmas joy, the comfort, the giddiness. I want to give her gifts, totems of potential, slices of the world. I want to fill her trolley with mad bastard levels of orange Matchmakers and I want to be there for it all.

SARAH NYATHIANG

My country, South Sudan, is the youngest independent nation on earth. We received our independence from Khartoum in 2011. However, we have been in a fully fledged civil war since December 2013 when the government and opposition forces tragically failed to go beyond their own interests and differences in a power-sharing agreement negotiated between the two biggest tribes – the Dinka and the Nuer. Five years later, over 400,000 people are estimated to have lost their lives with an estimated 4 million displaced from their homes – among these, only an estimated 200,000 people are being protected in one of the six Protection of Civilians (PoC) sites established by the United Nations Mission in South Sudan.

I am one of the 115,000 Nuer residents living in the largest of these UN sites, called Bentiu PoC, located in Unity State, in the north of South Sudan. Our PoC is surrounded by trenches and large mounds of earth, with barbed-wire fences on top and UN watchtowers. The PoC is divided into five sectors – each the size of fifty-five football fields and further subdivided into a minimum of seven blocks and a maximum of sixteen. It is in these blocks that each of the 18,500-strong households is allotted a space to build our *tukul* – a shack built of plant stalks, mud and plastic sheeting. The *tukuls* are hot both day and night and feel confined, but they are habitable and we feel relatively safe in them.

The year 2018 witnessed a peaceful Christmas celebration across South Sudan compared to previous years of the crisis – the coming of the leader of the South Sudan People's Liberation Movement in opposition to Juba to celebrate the signing of a peace agreement on 31st October, ended the five years of conflicts in South Sudan. Hope spread across the country – especially the Internally Displaced Persons (IDPs) in United Nations Protection Sites and refugees in the neighbouring countries. The celebrations across different protection camps brought a glimpse of hope and joy. Camps are known for their poor conditions and poor facilities and many wish to go to their homes and villages if peace returns to the country.

After the peace celebrations in Juba, people went to their homes with hope of a good Christmas and it was just some days to 25th December, the day when Jesus Christ was born. The traditional celebration of Christmas in South Sudan is like any other celebration across the world but there are some special things about this day. South Sudan is predominantly a Christian-dominated country with an estimated 80 per cent of the country's total population being Christian, but the greatest difference is when it comes to Christmas, as everyone celebrates this day, not only the Christians.

It was 23rd December, and in my Protection Camp, people were busy buying clothes and gifts for their family members and friends. Children were seen playing with toys and in a happy mood, local foods and drinks were offered for free by some families to their neighbours. The following day, 24th December, large crowds were parading in different colours – looking a little like a competition between the different denominations of the Catholic and Presbyterian churches. These crowds were marching in an organised manner with help from community security groups and the UN police and the camp was well secured. There was a lot of joy and happiness as children were singing 'Hallelujah, hallelujah, hallelujah'. The camp was filled with excitement and a hope of peace for the country as we were approaching the New Year. After the marching ended each denomination went to their separate churches, where they gave the Word of God to the people and encouraged each other to forgive one another and for peace to prevail in South Sudan.

It was a time for shopping – my husband and I went to the nearby local market and bought a big he-goat and other food items, along with some nice outfits for ourselves. The following morning, I prepared our breakfast and we joined the rest of the community in celebrating Christmas in one of the Catholic churches. After prayers I told my husband to come home with his friends and I also invited a few neighbours to join us in the evening to have some drinks and food. We prepared a good meal and we turned our music on and some women began to sing traditional Nuer songs and the atmosphere was good and I was so happy and excited, surrounded by the people who had joined me for Christmas celebrations. It became a celebration of Life – the best Christmas since the war broke out in South Sudan and a return to peace in my mind and heart.

On 25th December, almost everyone headed to the church for prayers service. Families were seen dressed in bright colours and the churches were full to capacity. The communities were also joined in prayers by some humanitarian workers and some peacekeeping groups. The whole prayers were all about peace and forgiveness of one another as people were approaching the New Year.

The celebrations in the Bentiu PoC camp were organised based on sectors and block by block. The head of Catholic Church in Bentiu PoC is located in sector four block seven and other sub-parishes from different sectors and blocks and they gathered together in prayers to celebrate the birth of Jesus Christ. The Presbyterian Church did the same thing where its members and other sub-churches under it joined them in prayers at the main parish in sector three block fifteen. Seven Day Adventist Church gathered in sector five block ten and Baba Juan groups gathered in sector two block two.

In my workplace we were able to organise a Christmas party, with all the staff from the Nonviolent Peaceforce (NP) gathered together, appreciating the good year of work we had all had, and celebrating together alongside some colleagues from different organisations within the Bentiu humanitarian hub.

After prayers different groups returned to their blocks with joy and excitement, praising and glorying God. During evening hours people gathered in different blocks in playgrounds celebrating the day and most people came from Bentiu Town and far villages to witness the drama and a traditional dance competition between the blocks.

The Christmas of 2018 witnessed the best celebration Bentiu PoC had seen. Despite all the suffering, family separation, tears and deep wounds in our hearts that the war in South Sudan has created, each day I pray to the God of infinite goodness to bring smiles and joy, so that we can rebuild our lives and our families. I thank my family and almighty God for the gift of life and hopes for a prosperous New Year ahead. May His name be glorified always.

Seann Walsh

You're going to have to bear with me here as, if I'm totally honest with you, Christmas was a rather depressing time in the Walsh household. My dad, who has been in constant battle with his demons my entire life (picture how Keith Richards might have ended up had he never learned the guitar), made myself and my brother very aware of the financial pressures of Christmas from an early age. It was quite clear that he'd rather have done away with the whole thing.

I don't think my parents have bothered with a tree for the past fifteen years or so. And as far as Christmas dinner was concerned, none of us cared much so my mum made her shepherd's pie, which it should be said was banging. We were never a family to have dinner around the table – we didn't even have a table you could have dinner around, so we'd all sit in the living room with our pie on our lap and stare in silence at *Home Alone*, which we could barely hear over the sound of my dad eating (now imagine an asthmatic T-Rex scoffing on a goat covered in Pringles).

I have for all of my adult life dreaded Christmas.

In the act of fairness, I thought it would be interesting to ask my mum, dad and brother to put in writing how *they* would describe a Walsh Christmas. This was a big move as we are not a family that communicate openly. Their contributions have been cut to keep the word count down.

BROTHER: PIERS – I hate spending Christmas at Mum's. No internet. No food. Stinks of cigarettes. Also middle of nowhere. Cold, no games. No DVD player. Just the television and the people (family) sitting next to you.

Last year, I thought: 'I'll have Christmas at mine this year!' I worked on Christmas Eve, then got home and tried to prepare for the blood-related nutjobs. Mum turns up with some essential Christmas food bits and bobs. Seann arrives with a brave face on, I see him getting out of a taxi regretfully and once inside he's already checking out the exits for a quick escape. First thing he says: 'Turn the music off, I'm hungover!!'

Dad, aka Michael Walsh, turns up (I was hoping he wouldn't).

So anyway, I prepared dinner. By the time I'd sat down Michael had finished his and left and gone upstairs without saying thank you. Seann was close behind. Mum and me sat there in silence eating the cold meal that didn't quite match the standards of those you see in all those Hollywood films and that you dream of as a kid.

It wasn't the worst Christmas I had. Far from it. The worst one was when Dad stole my Jack Daniels and drank it, then tried to get into a fight with me and my best friend. This resulted in the police showing up. I spent the rest of the day with my friend's family.

I hate Christmas. But that's because it's forced time with family. Maybe in the future if I have a family of my own, it will be different. I don't understand why we do it. We aren't a normal functioning family. So why are we pretending we are for Christmas. Christmas is pretending to like your family for two days. All I want for Christmas is to be left alone.

MUM: PATRICIA – We all gather on Christmas Eve. Seann and Piers take it in turns to have the Christmas hangover. Last year it was Piers, this year it was Seann's turn who arrived Christmas Day in the afternoon, looking very pale. He dived straight on to the sofa with the duvet and stayed there until Boxing Day, getting up once to gobble his food down. Piers watched the US *Office* all day while I was upstairs watching *The Wizard of Oz* for a change.

Boxing Day morning, Michael was looking out of the bedroom window to see if the buses were running and as soon as he spotted one, he was out like a shot. It was 6am. Seann called for a cab and moaned about how he was going to carry his big *Ghostbusters* poster, which Piers had bought him, on the train. We waved goodbye with two fingers to Piers, who waved back with two fingers. He couldn't wait to get rid of us.

We all decided we are not spending Christmas together again.

DAD: MICHAEL – On Christmas Eve, Patricia and I journeyed to Piers' place. He cooked Christmas dinner slowly on

Christmas Day, which meant that you could smell good food throughout the house.

There are four televisions in the house so we each went from room to room. One room became the 'light' room with comedies and talk shows. Another became the 'film' room where films were watched from start to finish. Pity the video was broken.

Boxing Day became a day of exits. I was first on the first bus.

*

Sarcasm there from Father Walsh.

So as you can see, not exactly what Santa had in mind. But I draw your attention to my brother's line: 'Maybe in the future if I have a family of my own, it will be different'. Since asking him to write for this, it has become news that he is indeed going to have a child and one of the first things he said was, 'I'm looking forward to Christmas for the first time.' It made me smile and I said, 'So am I.' The way he put it was, 'It will give Christmas a rebirth.' It will. And I too look forward to being part of that rebirth, to help bring this child up in a world where Christmas brings joy and happiness as it should and does. I cannot wait to see my brother happy on Christmas Day for the first time and I will be there with presents galore and without a hangover . . . Well, I will be there with presents galore.

SOPHIE THOMPSON

what does it mean to you, they asked?
wait a moment what do i remember first . . .
a photograph of a pink rug a flushed cheek and a wee
      red frock
a knobbly sock and soft strips of sherbety paper lick
      lick stick stick
fustle fustle like bird on a wing as you gather and
      bundle
a santa suit in the scottish snow
waking parents scare early with spooky shadows on a
      tartan wall
then it's being in a hall
a handsome kind wide hall with a real fire in a grate
and a gran from west ham going tut tut it's all too
      much
yardley lemon soaps on ropes
and musical crackers that make mum snort
me and my sis we'd hide behind our bedroom curtains
      make sticky things
plastic copydex and sweaty felt
loo rolls, great intent, and a sweet sort of secrecy

scissors with alligators' tiny teeth
sugar paper rolls & parched felt tips
mum would make meringues and brandy snaps curled
        around wooden spoon handles
and sometimes cry
she'd paint the brown paper parcels with poster paint
and the record of carols would play
stretched ladies warbling like kindness

auntie ele would have big gins and we could have
        bitter lemon
the colour of bank holiday weekends
it was the frantic shelf at the end of a tight rope
blood oranges in the corner of the boxing ring
hopes all wrapped in tissue soft to touch
sometimes we would sing
one awful november the dad
he died upturning a pyramid of hearts
& three hot salted ladies were found in a gentle flat
        pack flat
gone hot halls with hearths
all gone in a puff like rumpelstiltskin
and they did weep in pine cone shaped corners

unions would follow in blessed buildings
and the curious condiment
banged from its jar like ketchup
melted and re-formed like wax

shifting the underscore from before
and tiny little people miraculously become themselves
smelling of proper presents and powdered petals
cakes must be baked again mincemeat blessed and
        stirred
we spin a yarn and the cloth is very darned
and a rainbow of plastics emerge
& his mother dear and tense as tinsel
hiding in the garage for a fag
homemade pickled onions and halting shows of
        ancient slides
gulped down with spicy peanuts whisky in saccharine
        squash
where the comments crackle with repeat and comfort
        all replete
and the tide of the thames and the tide of the loch and
        the tide of the irish sea
foam in and out and in and out relentlessly
& husbands go to find other fables and nature tables
& blazing boys all big now burgeoning men
realising the magic must be made by them
& through the baubled din the dreadful quiet
deeply knowing as we step on the cracks that we are
        the lucky ones
with radiators roofs something still to lose

what does it mean to you they asked?
this intense confection this collision and confusion

LAST CHRISTMAS

what is this christmas thing?
it smells of promises and caramel
it sounds like a tiny storm in a tiny cave full of
      phosphorescent pools
and lonely people
it looks a little askance too shy to ask for a dance
handed down like unspoken wishes
like ancestors' strange patterned dishes
christmas the connective sinew
a wish from the bottom of tiny toe worn tights
that sweetness could be scattered soft as snow
make simply fair the catastrophic wonder of
      being human

STANLEY TUCCI

Each year as the days grow shorter in England, where I have now made my home, I cannot help but miss the winters of my childhood, appallingly more than a half a century ago, in upper Westchester NY. Our home on a cul-de-sac at the top of a hill was surrounded by trees, which by early December were almost always laden with snow. The ponds and lakes would begin to freeze over and the woods around us became studies in hard black and soft white, making them wonderfully mysterious and therefore more inviting than ever.

I loved everything about winter and I loved Christmas in particular. Our Christmases were joyous celebrations that to this day I still attempt to recreate.

Although my parents' funds were little more than limited, they made sure that our house was always elegantly decorated. My father, an artist and art teacher, had constructed a modernist manger out of scraps of walnut wood in which sat contemporary figures of Mary, Joseph and the Christ Child. Over the years other more traditional store-bought versions of shepherds, wise men and farm animals somehow made their way into our Gropius-inspired stable, but they always seemed to me to be unsophisticated interlopers. Each year when this homemade *presepio* (Italian for Nativity scene), the Christmas tree lights (the large, primary-coloured, hand-painted variety), the stockings and other decorative holiday bric-a-brac were freed from their crumbling cardboard boxes, I felt an almost overwhelming surge of joy. I knew that Christmas would transport us out of the prescribed, the mundane and into a week or so of undefined days filled with endless play.

As an Italian Catholic family, though now very un-practising, we ate only fish on Christmas Eve. Homemade food from recipes passed down over many generations was our daily fare but during Christmas this practice was elevated to even greater traditional culinary heights. My mother, an extraordinary cook, would prepare a meal similar to the one that follows:

APPETISERS: Shrimp cocktail; Baked clams;
Seafood ceviche; Stuffed mushrooms; *Zeppoli*

FIRST COURSE: Salt cod with potatoes,
green olives and tomato; Pasta with tuna sauce

SECOND COURSE: Baked salmon *or* Baked bluefish
with breadcrumbs; Roasted potatoes; Green beans;
Broccoli di rape; Green salad

DESSERT: Ice cream; Biscotti; Apple pie; Panettone;
Nuts and dried figs

Note: the above is not an exaggeration.

After this gustatory excess had ended and during the years when we still believed in Santa Claus, my two sisters and I would assemble a plate of carrots for his reindeer, as well as cookies and a shot of Scotch for Old St Nick himself. Although bits of cookies and carrots remained, the scotch glass was always empty. What a strange and wonderful coincidence that my father was and still is a Scotch drinker.[*]

Christmas Day brought yet another feast either in our home or, because Thanksgiving was celebrated with my mother's family, at the home of my father's relatives. The food rivalled that of the night before with *timpano* (a drum made of pastry filled with pasta, meatballs, salami, eggs, cheese and ragout) as the centrepiece of the meal with far too many dishes preceding and afterwards.

For me, Christmas always brought at once a palpable sense of excitement and a profound feeling of comfort. Time quivered giddily with the unknown as much as it stood comfortably still in the security and warmth of what was known.

However, even though I welcomed the daily routine of life being changed for a time to make room for what I have described above, what was most significant was that the entire spirit of life was also altered. For this limited period of time people were somehow capable of exhibiting kindness, courtesy and a generosity of spirit not normally seen throughout the rest of the year.[†]

[*] This tradition is carried out in my own home as I too enjoy a wee dram.
[†] This was most evident during my many years living in NY City where people's abruptness, or let's say, fucking rudeness, was replaced with an old-fashioned politeness, almost courtliness until the day after New Year's.

Although I know I can never recreate those Christmases of my youth, it is my hope that someday I, and all of us, will evolve to the point where we behave as we do during Christmas all year round. However, for now it seems that, although the spirit of Christmas is always lurking within us, we are destined to suppress it, consciously disable it or simply forget about it for eleven months. It may be that we need the calendar and/or the tawdry trappings of Christmas to remind us to behave civilly.

Yet I cannot help but wonder if, were these touchstones to disappear from our lives, we would innately know that we are meant to be kind to one another for at least a short period of time when winter pays us a crisp visit.

STEPHEN FRY

The British have a strange Christmas tradition.

In truth, many countries with a Christian heritage and background have strange Christmas traditions – strange to outsiders at least. Broom-hiding in Norway, the burning of a giant straw Yule Goat in Sweden, that fierce monster Krampus in Austria. On German television they annually broadcast an ancient British comedy film called *Dinner for One*; it features an unfeasibly drunk butler and his grand aristocratic lady. No one outside Germany and Austria understands why they do this; after all, the Germans and Austrians more or less invented the popular look of Christmas – 'Silent Night', snow, the decorated fir tree, Kris Kringle and the Germanised St Nicholas, Santa Claus. A slapstick British comedy seems a characteristic way to celebrate the season.

But that is Christmas. There is no festival like it for bringing out, not similarities and shared values, but differences and eccentric idiosyncrasies. There is a story, perhaps an urban myth, but let's hope not, that a department store in Japan, anxious to capitalise on the commercial opportunities the season affords but not quite understanding the details of the Christian story, once featured in its window a Santa

Claus nailed to a tinselled cross. It is certainly true that many Japanese, though Shinto by birth, like to celebrate Christmas with a Kentucky Fried Chicken dinner.

The British tradition, in my youth compulsory in the majority of households and still observed by millions to this day, was to put (the inevitably late) lunch on pause at three o'clock in the afternoon to hear the Queen of England deliver her Christmas message. Her words, usually pre-recorded in a study in Windsor Castle, were not especially memorable, original or stirring, but they served to cause the nation to stop and cluster around the television set, the nation's hearth. In my memory at least, the Queen always began with the words, 'Christmas is a time for families . . .'. My vain adolescent self, an incipient gay bohemian wastrel, far from the beau idéal of Family Values, would usually snort with some kind of haughty disdain at Her Majesty's homely platitudes. I look back at that silly self, in the warm bosom of a loving family, but thinking it all bourgeois and outworn, and I shake my head at my foolishness.

If you doubt the strength of the family, you only have to look at refugees. I come from refugee stock myself (as do so very many of us in the world) – my mother's Jewish parents, unlike most of their siblings and other relations, escaped the Nazi holocaust and made a life in Britain. I am not a Christian, but the foundational story of that religion is that of a refugee family. Another peculiar British tradition is a playing out of this truth. My first acting role at the age of five, in common with millions of British children, was that of a shepherd in my school's Nativity play. The following year I rose to the starring lead role of Joseph. As I showed off to my parents and the rest of the audience under a false beard and bizarrely unconvincing costume, did I know that I was playing a refugee? Did anyone in the audience consider that?

The force that drives the modern-day Joseph and Mary through the misery of holding camps, the terrors of trafficking, theft, abduction, rape and the horrors of all manner of violent depredation is family. The love a Syrian mother has for her children, the staunch devotion a Somali orphan shows for her helpless younger brother, these are the most powerful forces in the world. This force has to stand up to the sandstorm of the combined forces of greed, selfishness and indifference, but each birth and each child that survives is a Christ and each murder by violence or neglect is a crucifixion.

No, I am not religious, but I love and value the potency of myth, ritual and tradition. I love how the collective unconscious creates stories that, whether true in historical fact or not, are true in meaning.

I want to go back in time, sit with my mother and father and my brother and sister, give my silly conceited young self a sharp slap and tell him how lucky he is. But perhaps the best way to do that is to help remind the world that many of our brothers and sisters are holding each other fast in strange lands, dreaming of the chance to sit in a place they can call home.

You may well rightly say that all this wistful handwringing is not action. For another British tradition is to shake our heads, tut and complain, 'Why oh why do we proclaim peace on earth and goodwill to all men just once a year, why not every day?' But that is Christmas, as conflicted, complex, self-contradictory and maddening as all human creations. At best, like a reforming Ebenezer Scrooge, we can undertake to keep Christmas in our hearts every day.

Bless us all, everyone.

STEVE ALI

24TH DECEMBER 2015 – GOLD

I am twenty-three years of age. The temperature is below freezing. I am standing by a barrel of fire, warming my hands and drying my wet clothes. I shove a tree branch in to keep the golden embers glowing. I want to tell you there are chestnuts roasting on this open fire but I cannot. There's not much of a Christmas in a refugee camp.

My muscles ache from another in a series of failed attempts to cross the English Channel from Calais to Dover in the back of a lorry. A few British volunteers who are avoiding their family Christmases back in Blighty teach me and some other bedraggled refugees from Syria how to heat wine. 'Mulled', they call it. 'A waste of perfectly good wine,' I think. But Christmas is their tradition, not mine, so I smile and sip it politely.

'Happy Christmas,' they say. 'It's like Eid – except for Christians,' I explain in Arabic to those who don't speak English. They nod and smile, 'Happy Christian Eid'. The hot wine doesn't taste good but it warms the parts of me the fire can't get to.

We play Syrian music and dance around the blazing fire

under the moonlight, accompanied by the blinking blue siren lights of the French military police vehicles surrounding the camp and blocking so much as a sleigh ride to a life worth living.

Had the war not broken out in Syria, I'd almost be a qualified architect by now. Close to being a graduate of the University of Damascus, visiting building sites with my blueprints rolled up under my arm, respected and professional. Instead I am building makeshift shelters in a refugee camp wondering where my plans went.

We have nothing here but hope. But I am assured by the volunteers, who have celebrated Christmas every year of their lives, that hope for humankind is the true Yuletide spirit. They explain the baby Jesus was once a refugee running from a ruthless dictator too. He was born in a stable. A star in the sky guided the three wise men from the east to find him. I hope such a star is shining for me – and that I am such a wise man from the east and that someone will guide my way.

24ᵀᴴ DECEMBER 2017 – FRANKINCENSE

I am twenty-five years of age. I live in London in the spare room of a couple called Deborah and Tom who have welcomed me into their flat. I am invited with them to the home of their family friends in Lancashire. A country house called The Snug. This is my first real Christmas.

We catch the train. In our carriage, I am surrounded by excited families carrying bags of wrapped gifts. Out of nowhere I remember vividly a refugee family I met when I was walking across Europe. We trekked together for a week and I helped the parents carry the children. I get a flashback to a bitter, dark night when the temperature dipped well below freezing. It became clear to us that these small, confused bundles of children would not survive the night and so we asked the police if they could sleep in their car, so they wouldn't die of exposure, while we slept on the ground. I don't know where this family ended up. I feel a panic come over me on the train. Did they survive? Are they safe? Happy? Why am I eating gingerbread, heading for a warm, happy safehouse when so many freeze back in Calais? I can't focus. Deborah shows me a film called *It's A Wonderful Life* on her iPad. It's about a man who learns the art of survival at Christmas.

The house is warm and decorated with lights. The family are loving and generous and there is much food and laughter. All the Christmas customs are very strange to a Syrian who isn't Christian and wasn't allowed to watch Western films growing up. At Eid children are given money from the grownups in their family. At Christmas, children go to sleep thinking an old reverse-burglar man will break into their house and leave presents. It is not clear why the intruder doesn't frighten the children. His name is Santa Claus and he doesn't break in through the door. He comes through the roof! He leaves their presents in a giant sock big enough for a man's head. No one explains why. Everyone just accepts it.

I do not imagine Santa will visit me but in the morning there is not one but three stockings outside my door. It appears that various different people without consulting each other, have separately 'helped Santa' to make sure my first Christmas is special.

In the evening there is a big Christmas meal and everyone is dressing up. I iron a shirt. I make a note in my journal. 'Twenty-fifth December 2017. It is the first time I have ironed a piece of clothing since my exodus as a refugee.' I am starting to feel like a person again. A person who irons clothes and is given scented bath oil and chocolate and a pair of woollen slippers – that have all been chosen especially for me and not found in a bag of charitable donations.

I decide my favourite part of a traditional British Christmas is the way you welcome strangers like me into your families. If I were hosting Christmas dinner that would be the most important tradition to include.

I'm not sure about setting a perfectly good pudding on fire though.

24ᵀᴴ DECEMBER 2018 – MYRRH

I am twenty-six years of age. Deborah and Tom and I are packing to go to The Snug. It is my second proper Christmas and I feel like an expert. I have made many of my gifts out of silver because now I have a silversmith business in London, having learned to make jewellery in the Calais Jungle.

Our flat will be empty so Deborah has offered it to Refugees at Home. A young refugee fresh from Calais has turned up at the last minute to stay in it over Christmas by himself.

He's a solicitor in his twenties who's had to flee Kurdistan because he is gay and is in fear of being killed because people have found out.

He is going to his lawyer's house for Christmas lunch, but I suspect Santa Claus will not know where he's staying because he has spent the last three nights sleeping at Waterloo Station. I decide to be his secret stocking-giver.

I go to the shops and buy a stocking. Deborah explains when she sees it that I've accidentally bought a stocking made for a cat. 'He who lives a lot, sees a lot,' I tell her – an Arabic expression that sums up my increasing mystery at Christmas traditions. Inside the cat-stocking I put a globe of the earth so he knows the world is his oyster, an Oyster card so he knows the Oyster is his London and a pot of Marmite because I figure it's best for him to know the worst thing about integration right away.

I hide it and leave a message for him so that he finds it on Christmas morning. He is so happy, he cries a little. Sometimes it takes an outsider to really understand a custom. I realise now, the character in the Christmas story we should all aspire to be is the star in the sky that shines so brightly and hopefully – that someone else who is lost can find their way.

SVETLANA BENCALOVICI

Christmas is a time of the year that is difficult for me. I lost my father twenty-five years ago when I was twelve and a half – I have wished he was here every Christmas since.

But he gave a wonderful gift before he passed away. He showed me the importance of spending the holiday with the people you love. My father met my mother when he worked on a project in Moldova, far away from his home in the Ukraine. He settled in Moldova and I became the first of four children. Each Christmas we would make the long and arduous three-day journey on ancient and rickety trains to spend the holiday with his family in the Ukraine. We would spend the winter holiday season in my grandmother's tiny wooden house in a very small village called Plavie, in the Carpathian Mountains, where we were joined by numerous aunties, uncles and cousins.

These Christmases were simple but also magical. Winters brought deep snow that remained untouched as it piled higher. Groups of carol singers visited all day on Christmas Eve. There were no expensive gifts. But it was a time of celebration and relative plenty. We would eat special seasonal dishes and exotic fruit such as tangerines which were unavailable the rest of the year. It was a time of togetherness and, as I realised later, of unspoken love.

My father's death was sudden and unexpected. I had a brother and sister who were both babies. There is no welfare system in Moldova and his premature death coincided with the Russian withdrawal from our country – and an economic collapse. My family had no breadwinner in a country that offered no state support. School came second to helping my mother to earn money and I had to grow up fast.

When I turned eighteen, I left Moldova for the UK in the hope that I would be better able to earn the money to support my family. I had no English and no status. It was very tough. It would be twelve years before I could return home to Moldova with a British passport. In the meantime, Christmas would come and go in the UK. There were years I spent the day completely alone. Tears fall down my cheeks as I remember how I felt – far away from my family, with hardly a penny to my name, too broke to have a hot meal. I felt forgotten and beyond alone. But there were also years when virtual strangers would invite me to spend Christmas at their house, showing the sort of kindness that makes the human heart so unique.

There was one Christmas not so many years ago when I was able to reciprocate this kindness. One of my work colleagues, a man without family in the UK, told me two days before Christmas that he might be on the streets over the holidays, as he had been ordered to move out of his accommodation. I gave him my number and urged him to call me if it happened. On Christmas Eve he called – and came to spend two weeks in my humble flat. If I have learned anything, it is that it's a privilege to be in a position to give at Christmas time.

A few years ago I met a wonderful man I am now married to. We left London to live in the countryside, and bought a house where we could be able to offer protection and shelter: two of my siblings have moved in; my sister came to live with us from Moldova, with her daughters, my nieces, aged four and two who spoke no English. They now speak English with an impressive fluency. Christmas for them is as it should be – presents from Santa under the tree and treats galore. But surrounding them, as important as the oxygen they breathe, is our love, the love of a family that has been through so much but has managed to survive, so often with the support of kind strangers, and to make a life in a new country despite such difficult times.

Although Christmas will never lose its bittersweet edge for me, I also understand it is the time we see most clearly the things that really matter.

TINDYEBWA AGABA

My recollections of Christmas start at the age of seven: three days of festivities until we dropped off with exhaustion.

I was born in Gatuna, in the north of Rwanda, just a couple of miles away from the Ugandan border. Together with my three sisters, we lived with my parents in a beautiful oval-shaped, grass-thatched hut. Our compound also included a separate hut that functioned as a kitchen and grain storeroom; an open-air shower/latrine circular mud structure; and a kraal built with dry reed and bamboo plants where our goats and cattle lived. The yearly renewal and patching up of holes took place every December and I would help my dad to plaster all of our huts with cow dung. My dad worked on a tea plantation for a living. My mother sold vegetables from our farm.

My parents never got us anything new to wear until 23rd December. It was a treat we looked forward to all year long. When Dad arrived back from work, he would call us to sit down on the mat while he lay on his bed. He would hand each of us our new package. They were always Kaunda suits. You can't imagine the excitement! We never had access to any new clothes for the entire year until this moment. After trying them on, we would kneel and thank him a thousand times. We would then put them on for a trial run, to show them off to each other, before taking them off, folding them carefully and putting them under our feather and dry grass mattresses. We had to look after them. I remember how we would lie awake that night, looking at our new clothes and making sure the nibbling rats were kept at bay.

Early on Christmas Eve, relatives would arrive. Two uncles, three aunts and their twelve children, coming from our village and nearby ones. They never came empty-handed: some brought ducks, others brought sacks of sorghum and millet, yet others brought cockerels and a goat or woven mats and baskets.

To be brutally honest, it was exciting seeing our cousins after so long, but we hated their parents. They spent the afternoon picking on us: with my parents listening, furious with anger, they would repeat all sorts of stories – from us stealing potatoes from the neighbour's garden to begging for food from other students on our way to school or playing football instead of making sure that the goats grazed, even fighting with other children from other villages while we fetched the water. Both my parents would then subject us to cross-examination before giving us a hell of a beating. Even though I hated it, this was good discipline: I learned what behaviours were acceptable.

In the evening hours, the men would put up a makeshift shed where all the children were to sleep for the next three nights, since our hut was too small for twenty-two people. At Christmas, things sold out quickly and suppliers wouldn't come to our village until after Boxing Day, so my dad would send my older cousins to the trading centre to stock up on household essentials such as paraffin, salt and batteries for our precious old radio cassette, to blast out Christmas hymns and Congolese soukous music.

The women were in charge of preparing food and the local brew. Special foods, like ground nut paste, were left in banana leaves for the flavours to mix properly overnight. They would grind sorghum to make *Obushera* – a light non-alcoholic local drink – and put it in a huge, round pot to cool down. Then they would finalise what my mother had started a week ago – making a fermented alcoholic drink called *Omuramba* from a brown sorghum variety called *Omugusha*, an alcoholic beverage typical of where I grew up.

On Christmas Day, we woke up at 5am to get jerrycans and run to the well which was a good forty minutes away – three trips till the large container got filled with water. We never saw it as a chore because we were so excited about the new clothes we had just got and were looking forward to showing them off in church.

Meanwhile, my mother and aunts would start cooking the fresh food. The thrill of seeing rice was unimaginable – a once-a-year treat, only to be eaten at Christmas. Millet bread was baked and left to rest until after church. Chicken was prepared – again, the only time in the year we had the privilege of eating it. The boys were asked to chase after the chickens. Then my horrid uncle would slaughter them and pluck off the feathers. A goat was slaughtered too. Since it was a special day, both the goat and chicken meat were well seasoned and wrapped in smoked banana leaves.

We would dress in our new clothes to go to church. Every villager had to be in church. I remember that even at that young age, I understood how every single worshipper took part in the offertory to be sure that they were seen in their new outfit. The women's new hairstyles had a distinctive smell because they had been freshly done with special oils. The other thing which impressed me was the number of people who suddenly saw the need for wearing sunglasses in church – it never happened on any other Sunday!

After the service, we would head back home. Before sitting down to eat, another uncle, who owned an old Canon camera, would take photos. He would shout at us to get into position, pose and smile for the photos. No messing about because this was the only chance in the entire year to have photos taken.

The food was served on large trays: one for the male adults, one for the female adults and one for the children. We all sat around on the mats and scooped up meat, rice and chicken with our hands at a fast rate. For drink, I remember savouring Mirinda with my mouth wide open, but slowly, so that I could taste every bit of that liquid in my mouth. An absolute treat that I knew wouldn't happen again until the following Christmas.

After the meal, the adults would sit around and drink *Omuramba* from the same pot using long bamboo straws. All the children would head to the small village trading store, because it was another opportunity for us to show our new gear off. We would hang around and buy sweets with the pocket money our dad had given us according to our ages. We would return home around eight, to find the adults still drinking *Omuramba* and we'd dance to the drums our older cousins would play.

On Boxing Day, we were joined by immediate villagers: another chance to eat rare meat when a goat and a pig were slaughtered. While the adults ate and drank, we children would play and dance most of the afternoon and evening. We would all go to bed exhausted and belch throughout the night.

When I was twelve years old, I was abducted by the militia. I have now lived half of my life in the UK – sixteen years to be precise. My first Christmas here was very lonely. I was home-sick, cold and confused. Westminster Council had placed me in a Nigerian foster-care family after I had slept rough in Tra-falgar Square for several nights. The British Red Cross came round early December 2003 to give me my first warm coat and shoes. I couldn't believe that they were for free.

The only bright spot in my lonely life was going to the Ref-ugee Council day centre. They would offer English classes and hot food. There was also the opportunity of interacting with other newly arrived asylum seekers. One evening that Decem-ber 2003, the English teachers encouraged me to stay around so that I could attend my first communal Christmas party, an occasion that turned out to be a blessing as it was where I met my adoptive family. At the party, the man and woman who were to become my adoptive parents gently asked me what was I doing for Christmas, and could I join them on Boxing Day?

For the first time since I was abducted and kept in the bush, I experienced people celebrating with joy, happiness and laughter. And I was part of it. Although I couldn't understand everything they were talking about, it felt as if I had come home again, home at last.

There were presents, but the most precious gift of all was inclusion, acceptance into family life. I am hopeless at exchanging presents – it wasn't part of our culture at home – but I still treasure the Olympus camera I was given that day. Many more Christmases have passed under the bridge, but I still value the opportunity to be around people who care for me, to feast and to laugh and to share life's experiences with people who cherish each other's company.

TWIGGY

The strongest memory for me when I think of Christmas is the moment I woke up, as a young child, stretched out under the covers and my foot would hit a large sack (which was actually a pillowcase). Oh, so exciting!

It meant that Santa had been and left me presents at the foot of my bed, and yes, it also meant he had eaten the biscuit and drunk the milk which Mum and Dad had left for him. I would drag the sack into my parents' bedroom (where, as it was so early, they were still asleep), jump on their bed and very excitedly start opening the presents. Pure happiness!

We were a working-class family and my gifts usually consisted of a new outfit to wear and one or two toys. This was in the 1950s so it wasn't quite as commercial as it is now, but my mum and dad certainly made it magical.

We always had a Christmas tree and always a traditional turkey lunch with all the trimmings.

I know I was a lucky child, because although we weren't a rich family, I was surrounded by love from my parents and my two lovely older sisters. When I finally learned that Santa wasn't real it was devastating and Christmas was never quite as magical again, until I had my daughter and saw the joy and excitement of Christmas in her.

Because of my globetrotting profession we would often have Christmas in different places. Los Angeles never felt quite right as it was usually hot and sunny – weird! But the couple of Christmases we spent in New York, while I or my husband were appearing on Broadway, were fabulous. Ok, a bit OTT commercially, but, especially if it snowed, quite enchanting. Now, my husband and I have that magic all over again with our grandchildren.

If asked, do we spoil them? The answer is absolutely, and we have every intention of continuing to do so.

But the point of Christmas for me, that I learned as a child, is that it's not about money – it's about being surrounded by the people you love and who love you.

Valerie Amos

I spent Christmas 2014 in Thailand and on 26th December I was in Phan-Nga to commemorate the Indian Ocean earthquake and tsunami which had occurred ten years earlier. Nearly 230,000 people lost their lives. The human cost was immeasurable. Entire villages were destroyed and communities ruined. Families, friends and colleagues in the region and around the world lost loved ones. The devastation was overwhelming and the emotional impact, indescribable: that sense of the power of the elements that we could not control; the swiftness of it; lives snuffed out without rhyme or reason.

And it seemed particularly cruel because of the time of year. Christmas is, of course, an important religious celebration for Christians but also a moment of reflection for others around the world, as one year draws to a close and another beckons. The outpouring of support from people across the world was immediate and heartfelt as we were forced to think about our own lives, the things we take for granted.

At the commemoration ceremony and in conversation with people afterwards I was struck by the courage and bravery of the survivors. The determination to rebuild. The resilience needed to succeed. The commitment to remembrance. The boundless generosity. It led me to think about my family, to the connections between people around the world and the importance of remembering those connections rather than just focusing on distance and difference.

I was born in Guyana, a former British colony where Christmas was a mix of cultures, uniquely Guyanese. Grapes and apples, hardly tropical fruits, were a Christmas treat. Pepperpot, an Amerindian dish, was traditional Christmas morning fare. For my family Christmas has always been a time for coming together, of sharing – a time of generosity and thanksgiving.

When we moved to Britain our Christmases retained those elements. They were joyous occasions with friends and family, with shared jokes, a lot of laughter and of course endless food and drink. They were a celebration of cultures and a time to reconnect with other loved ones all over the world. They were a time to remember the past and think about the future. A time to celebrate achievements and give support where needed. We always thought about those less fortunate than ourselves. That was a mantra in our household. My mother never let us forget that there were millions around the world worse off than we were, and that we had a moral responsibility to help.

That desire for equality and for justice for people every-where has been with me throughout my life and has guided a lot of the decisions I have taken. In my time at the United Nations responsible for co-ordinating the response to humanitarian crises around the world, I saw the depth of inequality, injustice and sheer negligence around the world. The impact of state-sponsored violence, extremism, neglect, indifference. People abandoned, forgotten.

Of course, I knew this happened. I had been a politician. I had been responsible for the UK's aid department. But nothing had prepared me for seeing the scale of the impact of conflict and natural disaster week in week out. I went to so many countries including Syria, Pakistan, the Democratic Republic of the Congo, South Sudan, Somalia, Iraq and Yemen. I saw time and time again women and children traumatised by their experiences, as well as aid workers doing everything to help. I observed countries, on a daily basis, breaking their commitments to international humanitarian law, committing human-rights abuses and nothing being done about it. I witnessed political paralysis. But I also saw people who had fled their homes countless times and had nothing, do their best to support each other, and in so doing, giving each other a lifeline.

So many have become cynical about the notion of global solidarity, as we see politicians around the world turning to populism to garner support and paper over the cracks of their failure and inability to lead. My years at the UN taught me that most people want the same things: safety, stability, work and a healthy and happy future for their children. It's not too much to ask. Let's strive to achieve that not just every Christmas but during all the religious festivals for those who believe, and throughout the year for those who don't.

It's we, the people, that matter.

VICTORIA COREN MITCHELL

Here are ten Christmas presents that I remember.

1. A DOLL'S HOUSE.
At the breakfast table on Christmas morning, my father and his friend Basil seemed exhausted. They both smelt of whisky. Basil had a large plaster on his forehead. My father had an injured thumb. But the doll's house was *magnificent*.

2. A BOX OF MON CHÉRI AND A CHEQUE.
My great-aunt gave us the same present every Christmas. We paid the £10 into our Post Office accounts and it built up and up. We ate some of the cherry liqueurs. (I think we liked them. I definitely like them *now*.) It might not be what I would give a nine-year-old as a present, but she probably didn't know what to get. She didn't have Christmas as a child. And she didn't have her own children any more. She spent one Christmas in the camps. Or maybe it was two.

3. CHOCOLATE FOOTBALLS.
This was my brother's present, not mine. We sat under his desk eating them, long before breakfast time. It may have been five

o'clock in the morning. Or much later. But the time on the clock doesn't matter now, because it was thirty years ago and it seems to have lasted for ever.

4. A NECKLACE.
It was supposed to be a very special present, very expensive, very meaningful. There was a lot of talk about it in advance, a lot of excitement and special wrapping. But then there was a fight and it got ripped open too quickly, too carelessly. I think the circumstances were probably frightening. But what I remember is how sad it felt. You can't go again on that. You just have to wait a year and hope it's different.

5. A PAINTING OF NOAH'S ARK.
It was the biggest Christmas gift ever. It looked incredible under the tree. When I opened it, I was disappointed. I don't know what I was expecting, because a toy couldn't have been that flat. Perhaps I thought it would be a more colourful picture? It was dark; the rain clouds loomed much larger than the boat. The animals looked cold. But he was so proud to have bought it. It stayed on my bedroom wall for as long as I lived at home. I said I loved it. And I did, in a way.

6. SOMETHING FROM THE AIRPORT.
He died in November and we flew 5000 miles away for Christmas. I thought it might be a treat after everything. We bought each other presents from the airport. I can't think what any of them were.

7. A SILVER-PLATED ASHTRAY.

I found it in Portobello market. She loved it. It looked elegant, for an ashtray, and it had a sort of closing mechanism which meant you didn't have to empty it nearly as often as a normal ashtray. It was a long time ago. These days, I cough pointedly and open all the windows and wave my hand in front of my face. Sometimes I make her go and stand in the garden. But back then I was a smoker, too. I was new to smoking, so I knew (which I've since forgotten) that it was glamorous and cool. We were allies. She probably loved that more than the closing mechanism.

8. A BOX OF POLISH CHOCOLATES.

This was from a homeless friend. She left it with a mutual acquaintance to pass on, and the mutual friend forgot, and gave me the chocolates in March when they were past their sell-by date. But the card said, 'The spirit of sweet friendship brightens all the year', so it can't have mattered. This might be the most generous present I've ever received. I put the card on the windowsill, where it still is now, even though it's got a glittery Santa on the front and I'm quite superstitious.

(I also ate the chocolates. And I wouldn't have enjoyed them much more in December, because I'm not a fan of marzipan.)

9. ANOTHER NECKLACE.

The year we got married was the first year we spent Christmas together. Relatives crowded into our flat for lunch, then we opened our presents at night after everyone had gone. I still have the necklace but I threw the card in the bin. It was so lovely, I had to tear it up immediately. Otherwise I might find it again one day, when things might not be happy, and then it would be unbearable.

10. AN OWL.

Father Christmas gave my daughter an owl. The owl-shaped package ballooned out of her stocking. He was bigger than she was, but then, she was only one. In woodland terms, you might describe her as 'larger than a small owl, smaller than a big one'. As we helped it out of its paper wrapping, she hooted in greeting. Please God, may all her Christmases be safe. And consistent.

BIOGRAPHIES

ADEL BOTTERILL is a Crisis member from Neath in south Wales. She endured years of rough sleeping after a family breakdown led to serious alcohol abuse. Now in recovery and in her own property, she actively campaigns with Crisis on homelessness issues.

AIMEE MULLINS is an American athlete, actress and speaker. She lives with her husband, Rupert Friend.

ASHLEY COLLISHAW is a former actor, now an Anglican minister. He is currently vicar of a lively, growing church in Cheltenham where he focuses on the intersection between the Christian faith, creativity and wellbeing.

BEN ELTON is a novelist, playwright, television writer, screenwriter and lyricist. He is also a theatre, screen and TV director, a stand-up comedian and very occasional actor. He was born in south London and studied drama at the University of Manchester. He is married and has three children.

BILL BAILEY is a comedian, actor, musician and writer, best known for his live shows and work on television programmes *Never Mind the Buzzcocks* and *QI*. He is also the author of *Bill Bailey's Remarkable Guide to British Birds*. He lives in west London with a small menagerie of animals and humans.

BILL SCANLON was a director of one of the biggest post-production film companies in London, but became homeless after a divorce led to serious mental-health problems. He is now housed in London and is a homelessness campaigner with Crisis.

CAITLIN MORAN is an English journalist, bestselling author of *How to Be a Woman*, and screenwriter of the forthcoming film *How to Build a Girl*. She has worked for *The Times* since she was eighteen and lives in London with her husband, the journalist Pete Paphides, and their two daughters.

DEBORAH FRANCES-WHITE is a stand-up comedian, founder of *The Guilty Feminist* podcast, screenwriter and Amnesty International ambassador.

SIR DEREK JACOBI CBE is an English actor and stage director. In addition to being a founding member of the Royal National Theatre, he has also enjoyed a successful television and film career.

EMILIA CLARKE is an English actress who rose to international fame for her breakthrough role as Daenerys Targaryen in the HBO fantasy television series *Game of Thrones*.

EMILY WATSON OBE is an English actress who has appeared in numerous acclaimed films including *Breaking the Waves, Punch Drunk Love* and *Chernobyl*. She lives with her husband and children in London.

DAME EMMA THOMPSON DBE is one of the UK's most acclaimed actresses, screenwriters and activists. She is the president of the Helen Bamber Foundation, a patron of the Refugee Council and the Elton John AIDS Foundation and an ambassador for Action-Aid. She splits her time between London and Scotland with her husband, Greg Wise.

BIOGRAPHIES

GRAHAM NORTON is a broadcaster and a bestselling writer. He presents *The Graham Norton Show* on BBC1 and has a weekly show on BBC Radio 2. Born in Dublin and raised in West Cork, Norton now lives in London.

GREG WISE is an actor, filmmaker and writer. He is married to Emma Thompson, with whom he shares two children.

IAN RICHARDS first volunteered with Crisis in 1992, becoming Head of Christmas in 2014. He lives and works in London.

JADE JACKSON grew up in Uganda and came to the UK as a refugee in July 2001.

JO BRAND is an English comedian, writer and actress who used to work as a psychiatric nurse. She lives with her family in England.

LORD JOHN BIRD MBE was homeless for two years at the age of five, and then lived in an orphanage until he became a butcher's boy. He was a founder of *The Big Issue*.

JORDAN STEPHENS is a writer, actor and musician. He is one half of British duo Rizzle Kicks.

JOSH ROGERS has been volunteering with Crisis since 2014. He lives in London with his wife who is also a volunteer. Josh is now a Lead Volunteer, and for the rest of the year works in education technology.

KATE PARROTT is a born-and-bred southerner who is happily living with her husband in the north-east of England. She is a proud heart-transplant recipient, enjoying life to the full, travelling the world and making memories along the way.

KATY BRAND is an English actress, comedian and writer, known for her series *Katy Brand's Big Ass Show*.

LAILA OMAN was born in Egypt in 1990. She works as a painter in Berlin.

LYSE DOUCET OBE, CM is the BBC's chief international correspondent. Born in Canada, she now lives in London.

MAHA THAHER was born in Palestine in 1989. She holds a BA in English and Translation from Birzeit University and an MA in Conflict Resolution from UMass Boston. She is passionate about children and youth education, female empowerment and peace-building through community development.

DR MALCOLM WALKER was born in Latin America. He is a consultant in a major central London teaching hospital. He lives with his wife in south-west London.

MEERA SYAL CBE is a British Indian actor and writer.

MERVYN BROWN MBE was born in 1927 and was awarded his MBE in 2006 for services to people with heart problems in Harrow and Brent. He lives in Pinner with his wife.

MERYL STREEP is a multi-award-winning and internationally acclaimed American actress. She is known for her work in such diverse films as *Sophie's Choice*, *The Deer Hunter*, *The Devil Wears Prada* and *Mamma Mia!* She lives in New York City.

DR MICHAEL KORZINSKI is a Trauma and Psychosocial specialist based in London, but working internationally, with survivors of torture, human trafficking and other forms of human cruelty. He also advises police and lawyers in the criminal justice sector and enjoys collaboration with other professionals.

MIKE TUOHY BEM began volunteering with Crisis in 1979. He met his wife, Michelle, there and they have a fifteen-year-old son (called Andrew). Mike is a Director of Facilities Management at Knight Frank and the family live in Hertfordshire.

NAWA MIKHAEIL was born in Baghdad, Iraq. She works at the International Organization for Migration (IOM) in a programme that works to reunite refugee families with their nuclear-family members in Germany. She lives in Erbil.

NI NI MYINT has been working in the development and humanitarian sector over the last ten years. She is Head of Programmes in Christian Aid. Prior to this she was a history professor at the Theological Institution in Mandalay. She lives in Myanmar.

OLIVIA COLMAN CBE is an award-winning English actress. Between roles in critically acclaimed television shows *Peep Show*, *Broadchurch* and *Fleabag*, she has starred in films as varied as *Hot Fuzz* and *The Favourite*, for which she won the Academy Award for Best Actress. She lives with her husband and their three children in London.

PAUL FEIG is an American actor, film director, producer and screenwriter. He is best known for directing films including *Bridesmaids* and *Ghostbusters*, and for creating the TV series *Freaks and Geeks*. He is also the director of *Last Christmas*.

PHYLLIDA LAW OBE is a Scottish actress and writer. She lives in London and is the mother of Emma and Sophie Thompson.

RICHARD AYOADE is a multi-award-winning comedian, actor, writer and director.

ROSE NAM was born and brought up in Uganda. She came to the UK as a refugee in 2015. She now works as a Community Development Practitioner.

RUPERT FRIEND is an English actor, director, screenwriter and producer. He is best known for his role as Peter Quinn in *Homeland*, for which he was nominated for an Emmy in 2013. He lives with his wife Aimee Mullins.

SADIE HASLER is a multi-award-winning columnist, playwright and actor. She is co-Founder and Artistic Director of the theatre company Old Trunk. She lives in Westcliff-on-Sea with her daughter and her partner.

SARAH NYATHIANG is South Sudanese and specialises in Gender Based Violence issues for a number of international organisations including Nonviolent Peaceforce, a global NGO, and the IRC.

SEANN WALSH is an English comedian who appears regularly on television. He lives in London.

SOPHIE THOMPSON is an actress who has worked in theatre, television, film and radio – she also likes to try and write sometimes. She lives in north London with her two sons.

STANLEY TUCCI is an award-winning actor, writer, producer and director. He lives with his wife and their five children in London.

STEPHEN FRY is an English comedian, actor and bestselling writer. He and his husband live in London.

STEVE ALI is a Syrian refugee who studied architecture at the University of Damascus. He lived in the Calais Jungle refugee camp, built many of the structures and fought fires. Now living in London, he is a writer, silversmith and interpreter for BBC, NBC Universal and Refugee Action.

SVETLANA BENCALOVICI was born in Moldova in 1981. She moved to London when she was eighteen. She now lives in Lincolnshire with her husband. Svetlana works as a civil servant for the RAF.

TINDYEBWA AGABA was born in Rwanda. He escaped for England when he was sixteen, where he was homeless until he met Emma Thompson and Greg Wise at a Refugee Council event. He is now their adoptive son. He works as a human rights and legal humanitarian activist and lives in London.

DAME TWIGGY LAWSON DBE is an award-winning actress, model, singer and fashion designer. She rocketed to fame in the mid-Sixties, becoming the world's first supermodel and a British cultural icon. She lives in London with her husband.

BARONESS AMOS CH, PC is a British politician and diplomat who served as the eighth UN Under-Secretary-General for Humanitarian Affairs and Emergency Relief Coordinator. She lives in London.

VICTORIA COREN MITCHELL is a writer, presenter and poker player. She presents *Only Connect* on BBC2, *Heresy* and *Women Talking About Cars* on BBC Radio 4, is the author of three books and lives in London.